We All Gotta Go Sometime

ISBN-13: 978-0-9972920-5-3
ISBN-10: 0- 9972920-5-9

Cover design by LaDawn Nichols

First printing, December, 2016

Disclaimer: The vast majority of the photos contained in this volume are of public ladies' restrooms. Most were taken at eating establishments. Except for one or two that are used here with permission, all photos were taken by the author.

Published by:

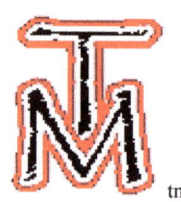

ThomasMax Publishing
P.O. Box 250054
Atlanta, GA 30325
www.thomasmax.com

We All Gotta Go Sometime

One Woman's Obsession with Public Restrooms

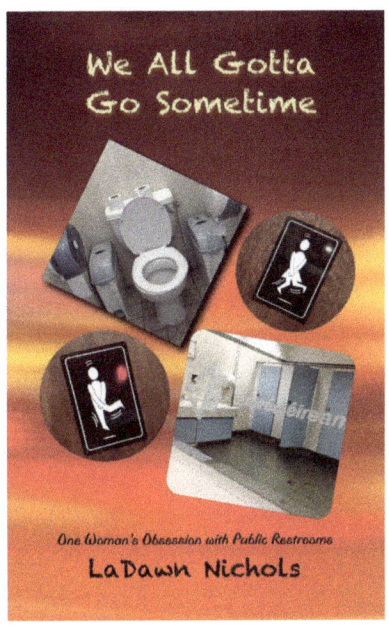

LaDawn Nichols

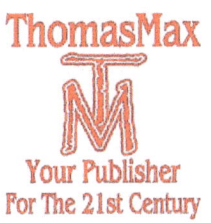

ThomasMax

Your Publisher
For The 21st Century

INTRODUCTION

Shortly after successfully toilet training my youngest son, I found myself wishing I hadn't. Oh not for the reasons you may be thinking of. I certainly was not the sappy mother whose heart was breaking at her baby boy's next step toward complete independence.

Once my son was toilet trained I envisioned a bit of my own freedom and certainly lighter loads as I would no longer be carrying diapers and wipes every time we left the house for more than five minutes. But, in completing yet another time honored motherly duty I unintentionally trapped myself. Every outing would take twice as long now, because there seems to be an allure to never before seen public restrooms. Something I failed to recognize back then.

Every time we went somewhere that my son had not utilized the facilities in, he suddenly and desperately needed to use the restroom. It was an almost Pavlovian dog response. I only went to the grocery store to pick up a gallon of milk, but my son released he hadn't ever been to the restroom there before and did the pee-pee dance until I took him.

Anticipating that he would need to go as soon as we got some place I highly encouraged, okay I bribed him, to go to the bathroom before we left the house. Arriving at the same grocery store a second and third time, without having to be led by a running toddler to the restroom made me think I had successfully solved the problem.

Not so. On the very next trip, to a similar, yet differently located grocery store we made the mad dash to the ladies', even though he had emptied his bladder fully prior to leaving the house just ten minutes before. And so it began, the great restroom appraisals.

Thankfully, this only lasted until he was about five years old. The necessity of the room seemed to have dimmed its charm. Or perhaps the gents' isn't as fascinating as the ladies'. By age five he was big enough for his ten-year-old brother to take him into public restrooms rather than mom.

Fast forward thirteen years and now this same child will only use a public restroom if he is busting a gut. However, his mom now wants to visit each new location, no matter how little she really has to go, and always with her phone in hand.

It seems I have developed a very strange fetish. Restroom pictures, literally, pictures of public restrooms. Beginning on my trip to the UK in 2013, I have taken pictures of many of the public restrooms I have visited. The practice seemed to naturally continue when I returned home as I found myself snapping pictures in loos all around my city, and even at rest areas along our road trips to visit my parents. I think I have it bad! I mean what sane individual would hang about in a public restroom, waiting for it to empty just to be able to take a picture. *Raising my hand sheepishly.*

I always have my phone in my pocket. This makes for very easy access to capture the moment, no matter how yellow tinted everything is before the shutter snaps.

I hope you'll enjoy my little photo journal. Now if you'll excuse me, with all of this toilet talk, I need to "Skip to the Loo, My Darlin'."

--LaDawn Nichols

For all of my family and friends who listened to the explanation of my newfound fetish, without judgment, and who actually encouraged me to continue

In the beginning, there was….

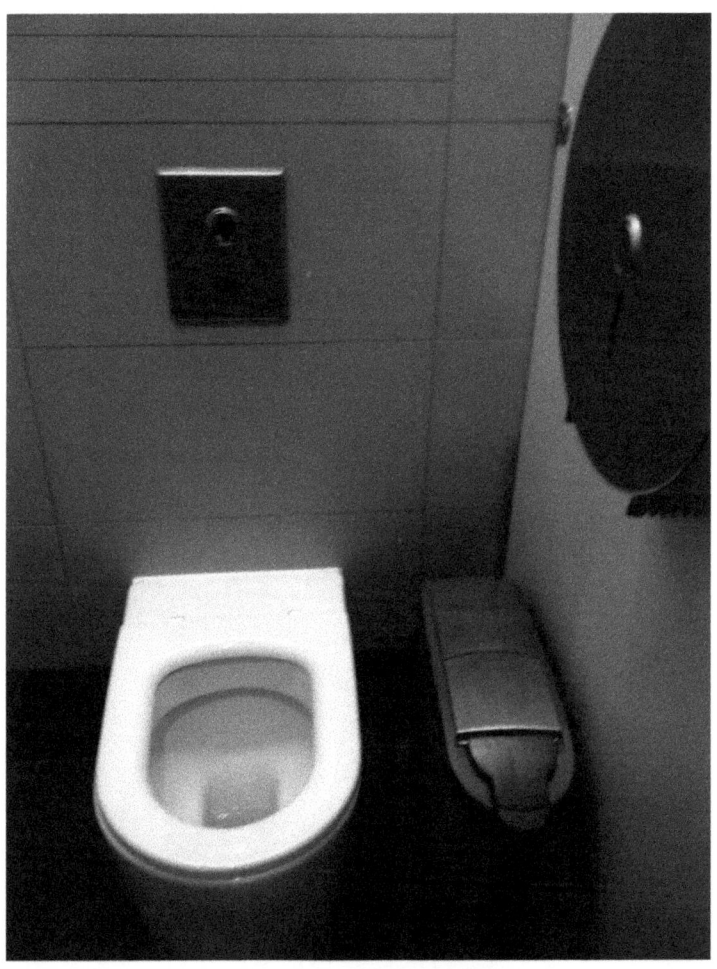

…this toilet.

I was on a school trip with my oldest son, a nine-day whirlwind tour of Dublin, Wales, and London. We had just landed in Dublin International airport, and while standing around the luggage carousel I felt nature's urgent call. So I made a beeline for the toilets only to be stopped by this befuddling site. My eyes darted everywhere, my mind raced. Where's the tank!? Where's the flush handle!? Never mind, my need to get the yellow out of my eyes was outweighing my need to know how the thing functioned. Thankfully I worked it out in the end. But I had to take a picture. And that is how this whole thing started; out of a moment of jetlagged confusion on a nature call.

* * *

It's amazing the things one finds in public restrooms, other than stalls of toilets of various shapes and sizes. This for instance, hanging on the wall perpendicular to the sink and mirror.

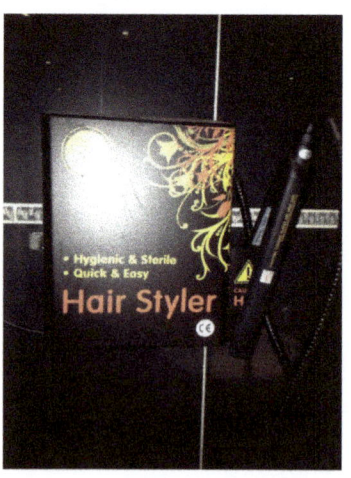

Hygienic and sterile. Really!?

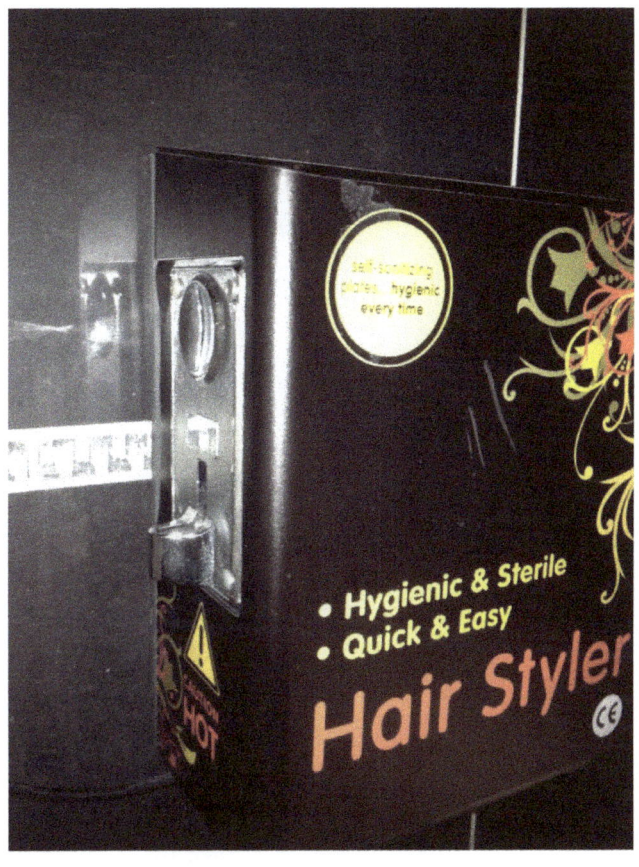

* * *

Walking around in central London I came upon this monolith clearly designed to accommodate vertically gifted males (see page 4):

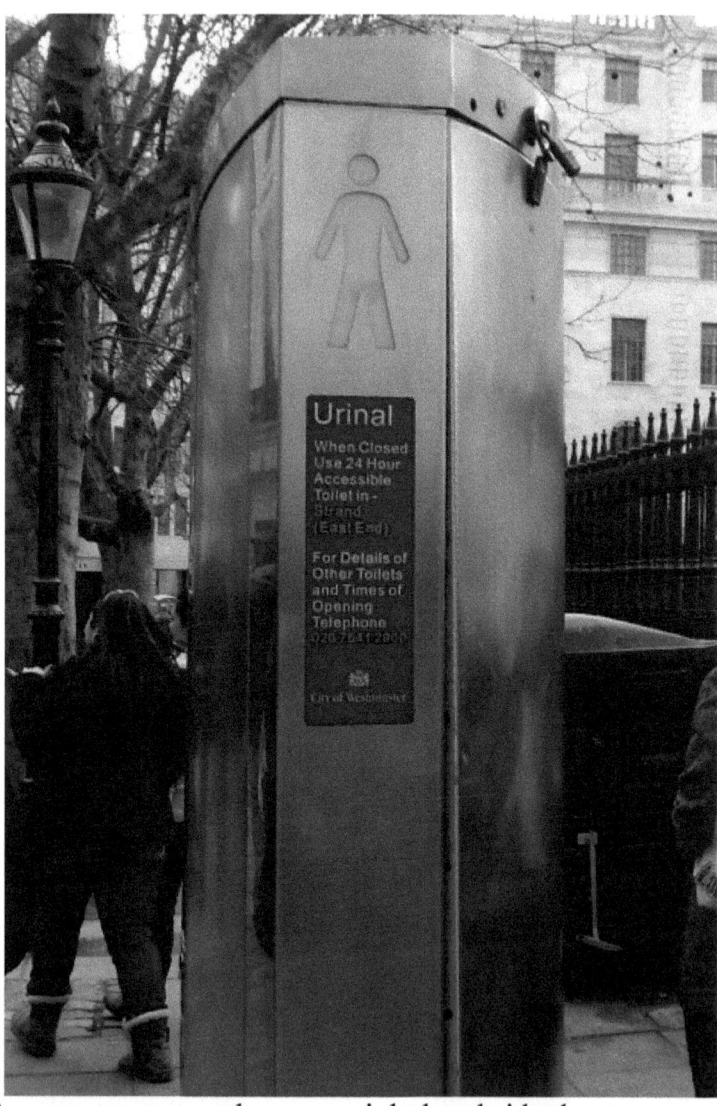

As you can see on the upper right hand side the structure has a solid bolt lock. This location was clearly closed on Easter Sunday morning. Poor chaps. I hope they are able to hold it all the way to Strand.

Mirrors…..

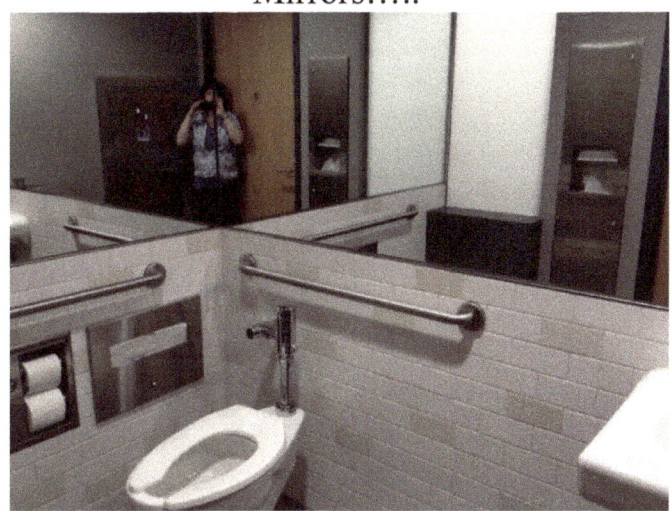

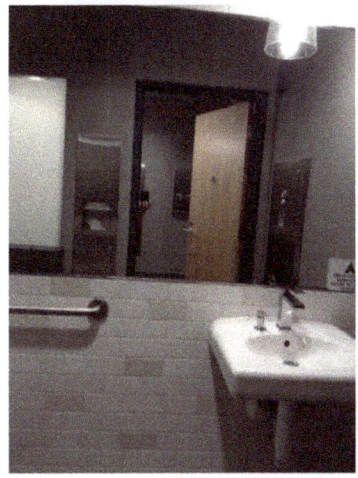
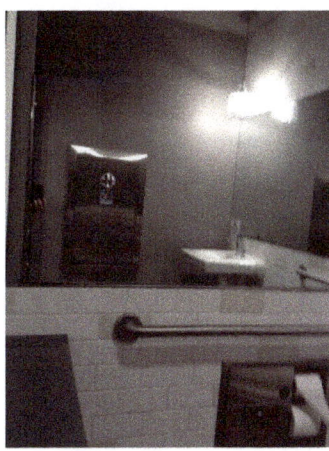

…all around! Makes one wonder what they expected their patrons to be doing in this single seat stall.

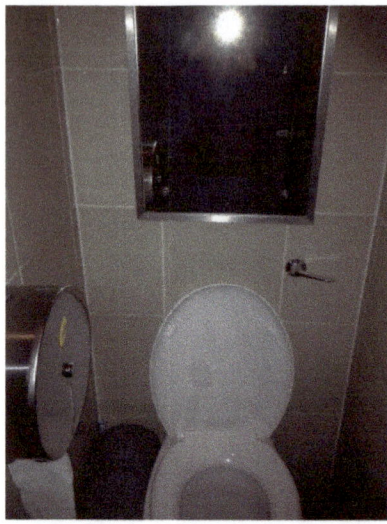

Why would one need a mirror IN the stall, behind the throne?

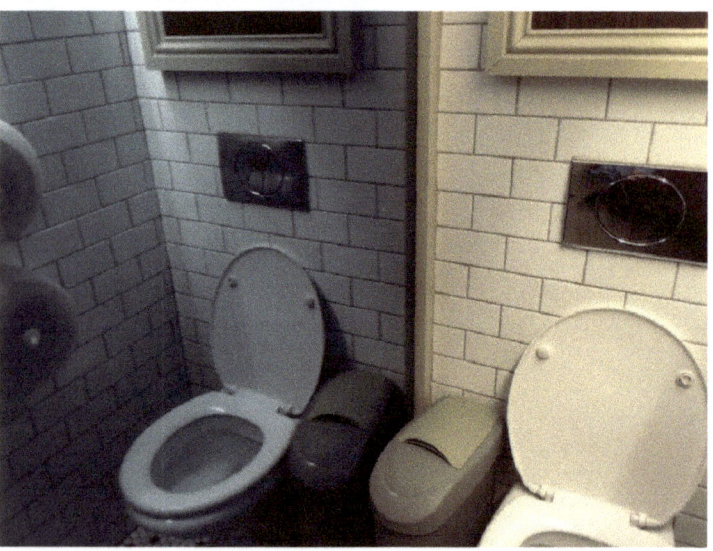

If you didn't have personal hang ups before, watching yourself pee just may do it!

You know, mirror placement really should require a science degree for some establishments. Here are too fine examples of putting the mirror too low (I could see myself from the shoulders up while sitting on the toilet, and I'm short!) …

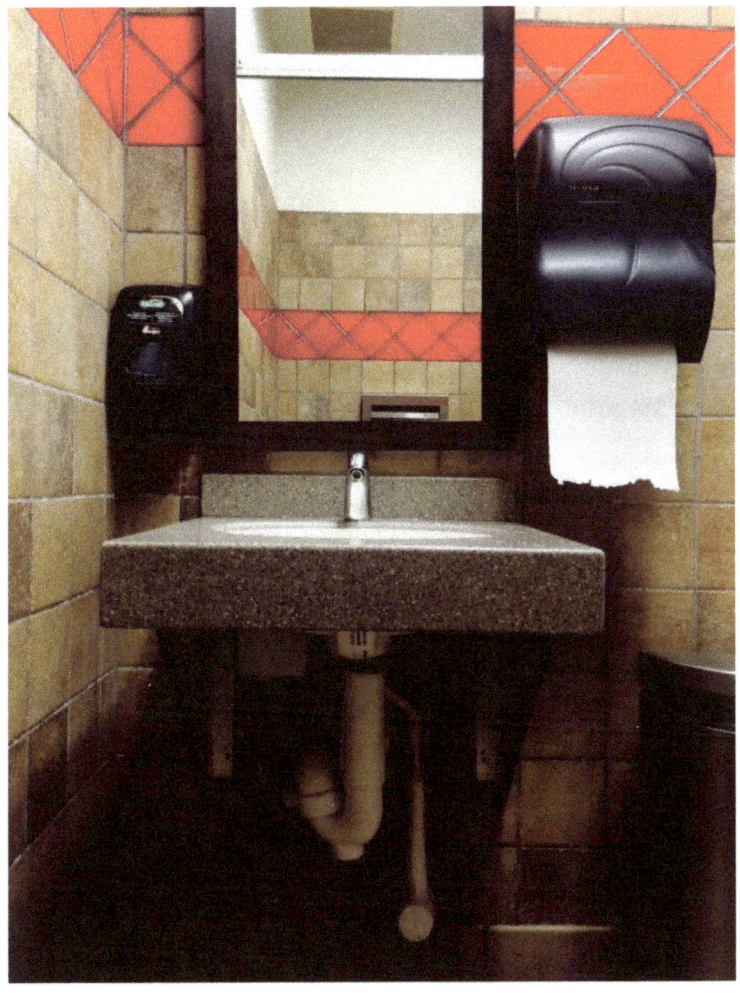

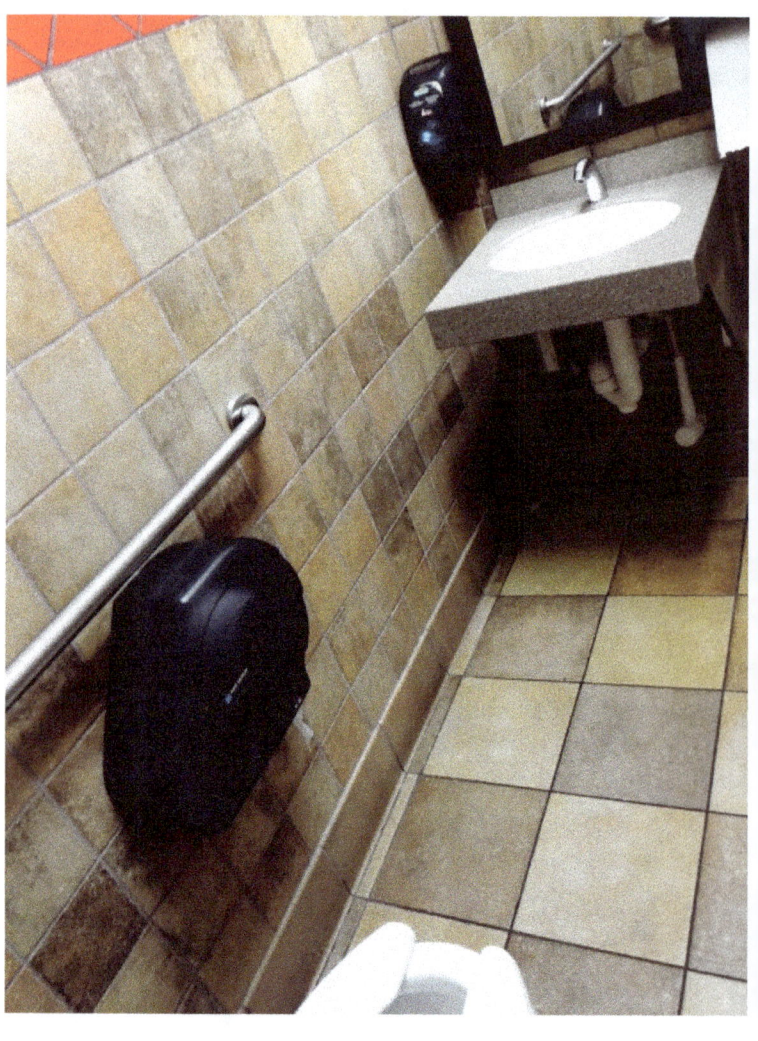

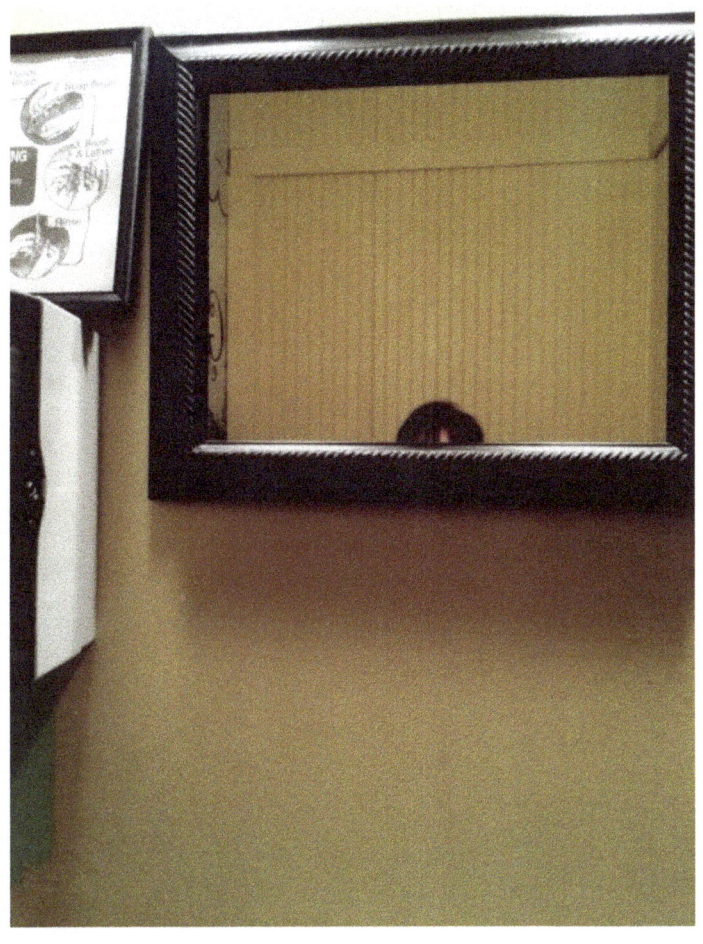

…and too high (even in 2 ½" heels I was not tall enough to see my face).

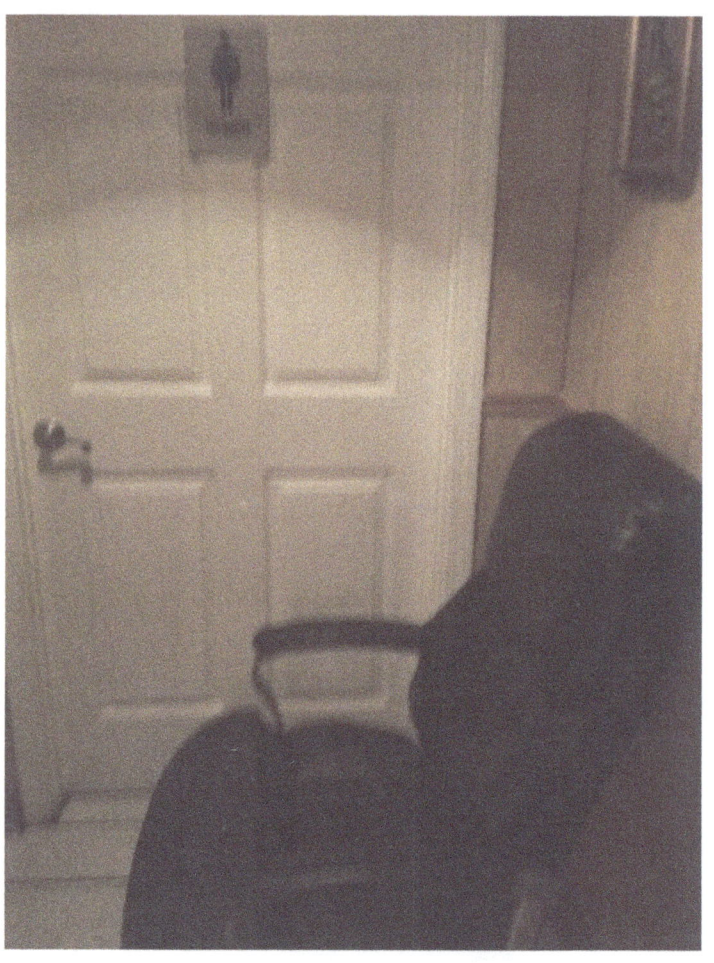

A chair, precariously perched outside the ladies powder room. Whatever was that for? Had they run out of storage space? Oh no, it served a purpose.

I was just snapping the inside picture when a lady walked in on me. Oh yes, I had the door locked, but it was obviously defective. We laughed about it for a few minutes then tested the door. The lock was virtually ineffectual. She asked me to call her husband over to stand guard for her. I'd never seen her before in my life! How was I going to find her husband? Luckily the chap in question wandered by before she popped inside and she gave him the instructions. He and I looked at the chair a moment then, he smiled and sat right down. I don't even remember why I was so keen on snapping this bathroom. It wasn't all that remarkable. Still, it was early days in my obsession.

* * *

A reader of my blog sent this one in, after telling me I was a weirdo of course. This is a men's restroom at a restaurant he visited on his summer holidays. What do you think the lever under the edge of the seat is for?

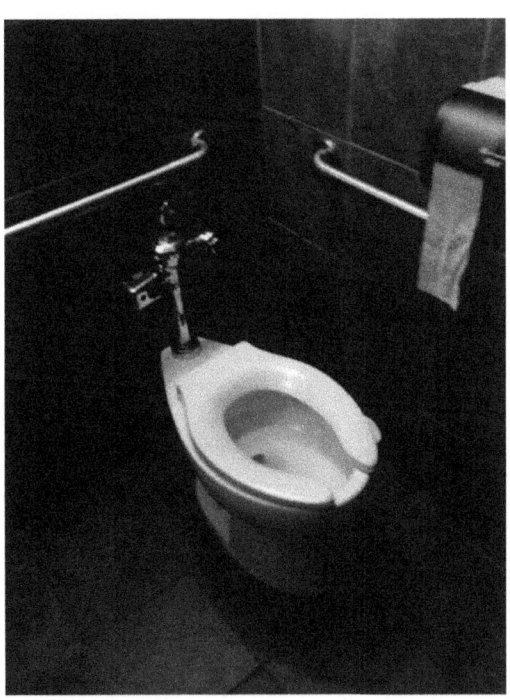

He generously sent over two. Here, wee little ones can feel like a big kid.

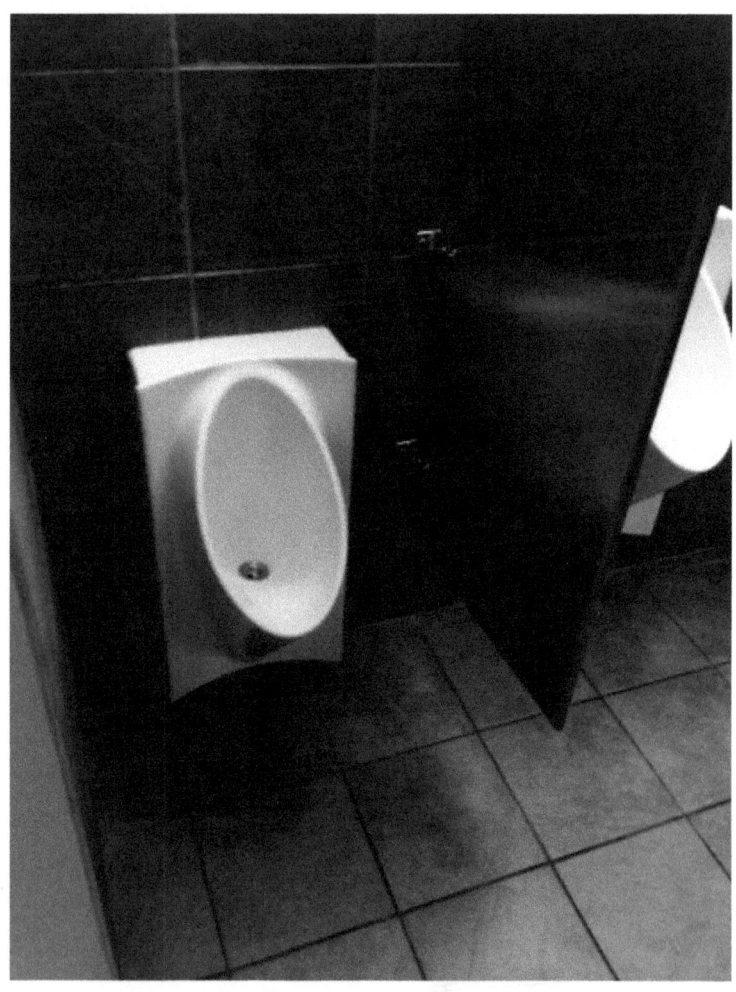

My own son has even gotten into the act. While I did ask him, (okay, so I nagged…a little) to take a picture of one of the men's public toilets in Ireland (see page 39), this picture was a gift. He took it on his own and showed it to me when he got home from his lunch out with his dad. I had my head buried deep in lesson planning for the coming week and was not in the best of moods when he walked in. But, his briar-eating grin radiated the room as he shoved his phone under my nose. He seemed so proud to show me the nerve he had exhibited that my heart melted. My teacher's manuals now set aside; he began to tell me how he came to take the picture as we added it to my collection.

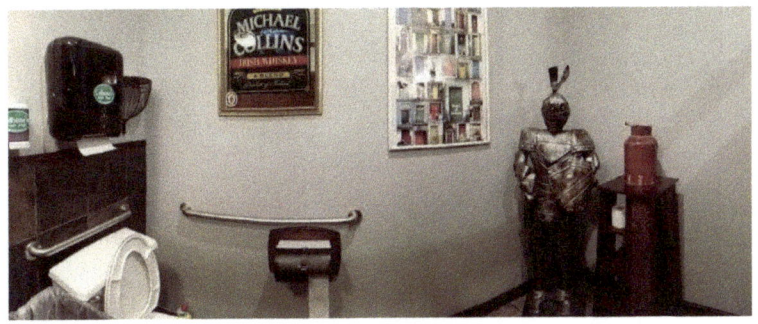

Is it just me, or is it kind of weird that the paper towel dispenser is above the toilet? Is toilet paper not enough for some?

At a local bar/restaurant, the owners seem sensitive to a lady's needs. They've provided a "bad date backdoor" escape route.

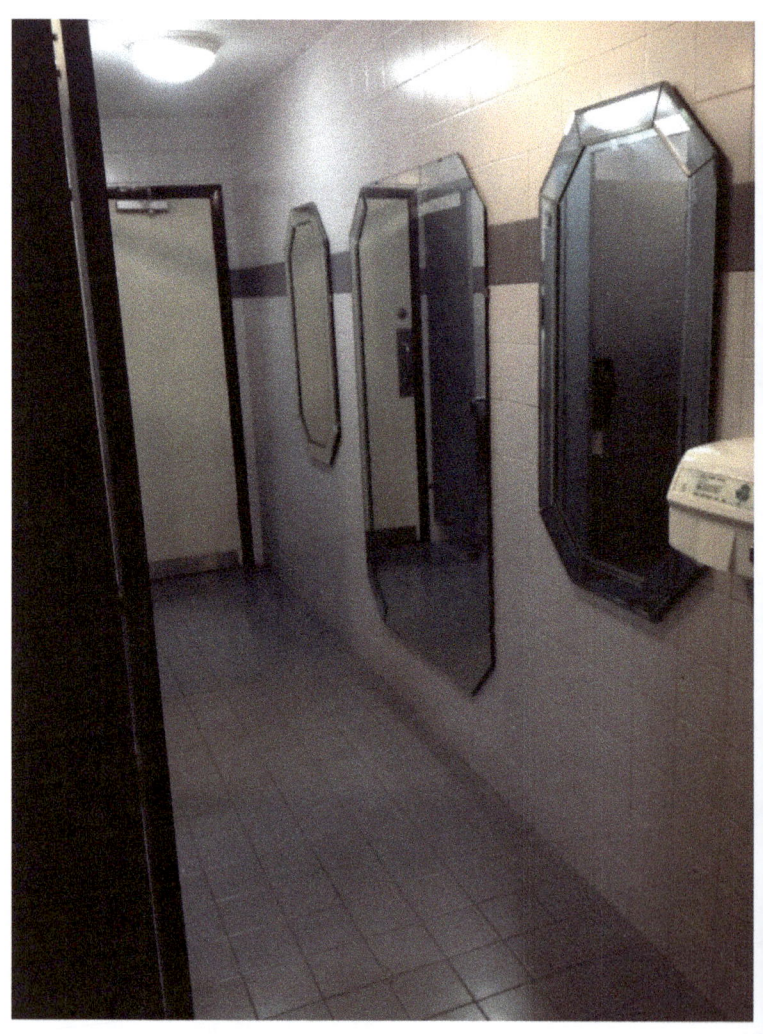

Apparently they want their lady patrons to be prepared for every eventuality by providing a variety of bathroom tissue placements. I suppose one never knows exactly what condition they will be in when the moment arrives nor how well they will be able to reach the sacred scroll from certain positions.

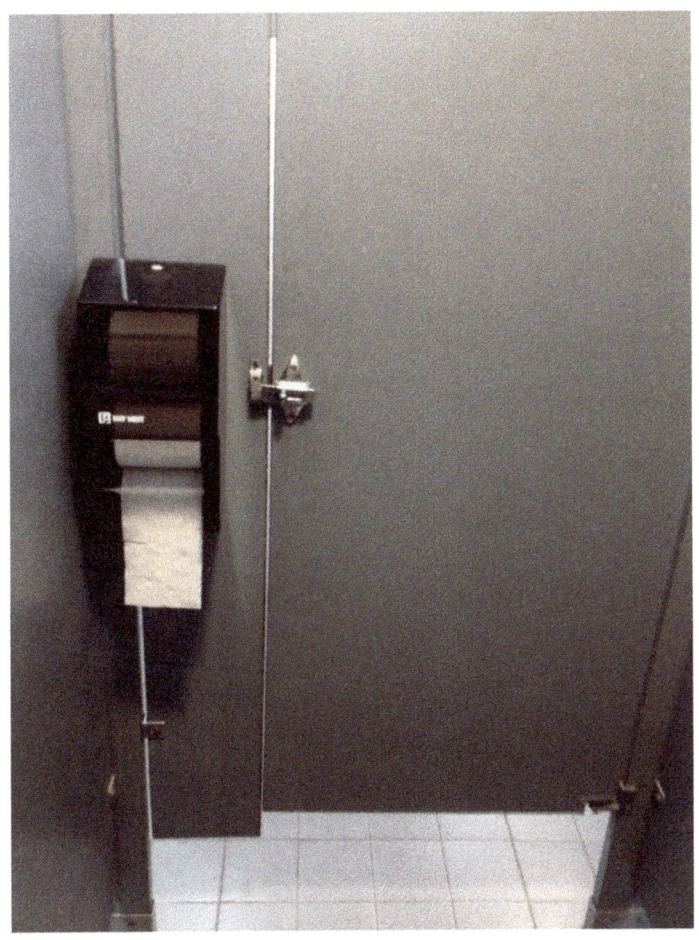

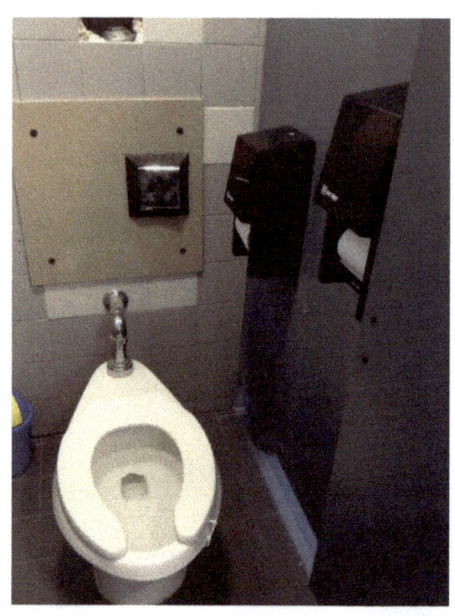

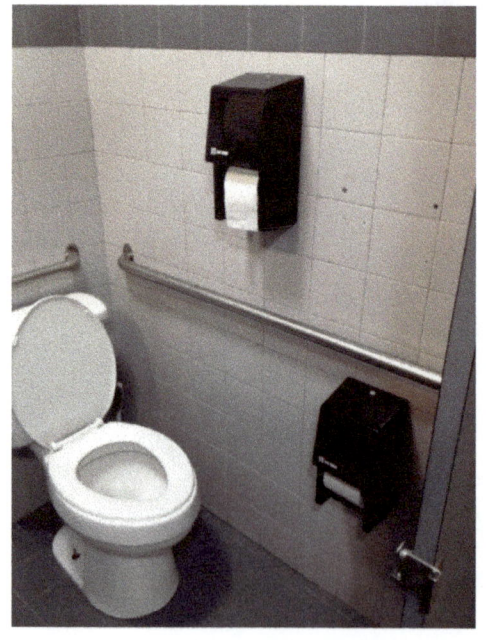

Irish pubs know how to keep their ladies though. Here we have barely enough room to move while doing our business

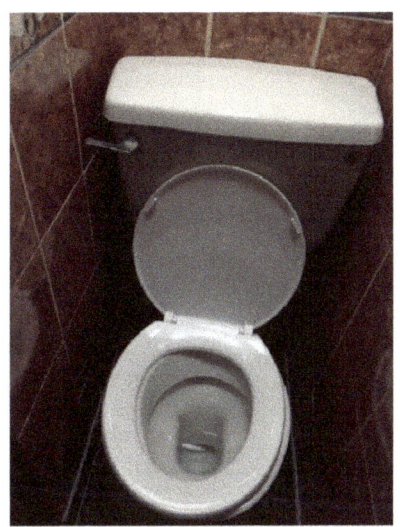

and here there are bars preventing any egress other than the door you came in.

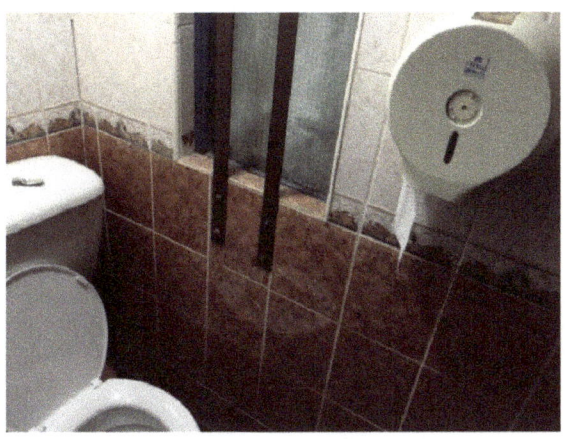

I told you I was that crazy lady taking photos in rest area restrooms! This restroom was along Interstate 10 somewhere in Florida or perhaps Alabama.

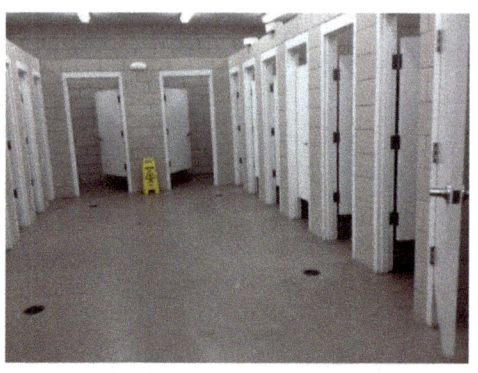

Here we had the most stall privacy I have ever seen in America. The sink piping was even covered.

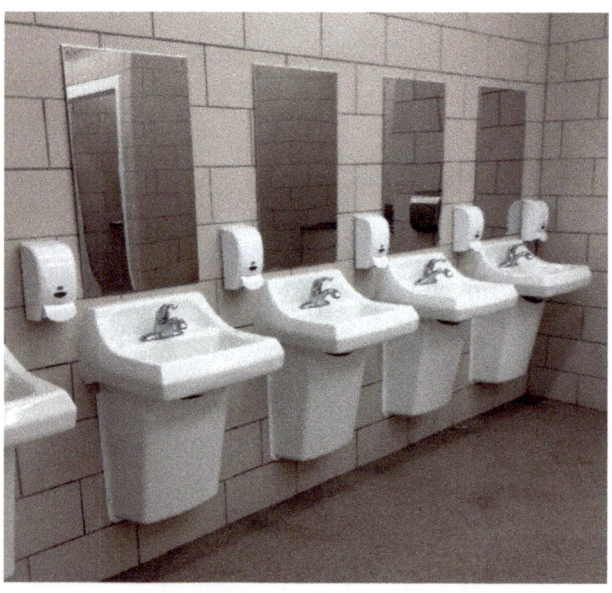

I thought I was back in Europe

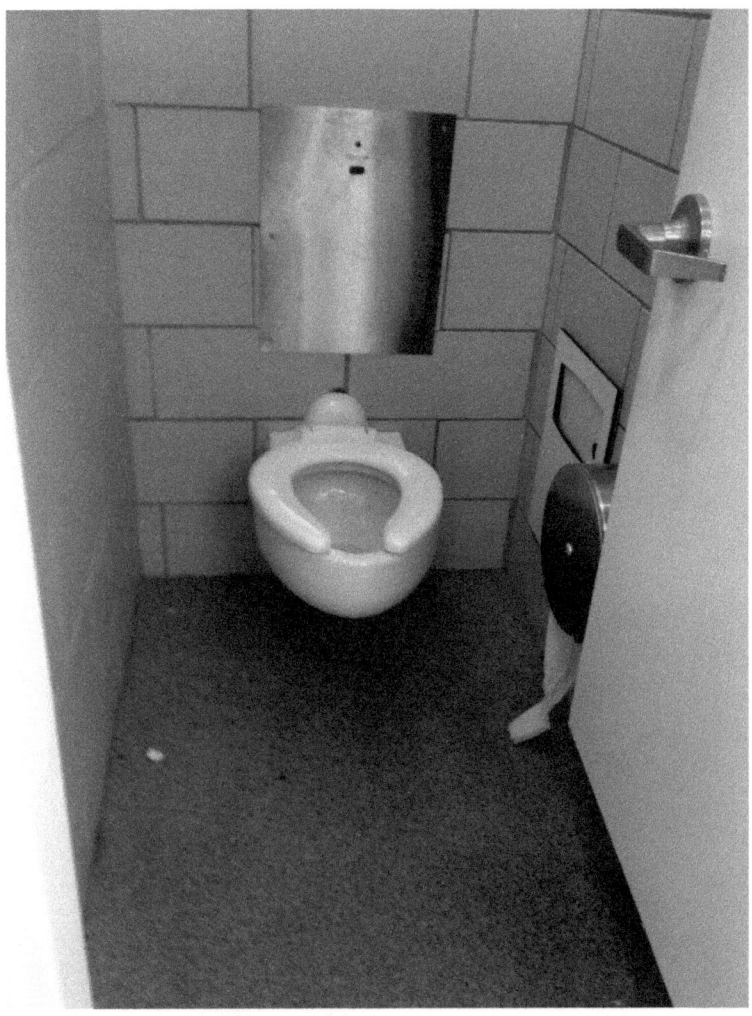

This nice rest area restroom came with very helpful warnings.

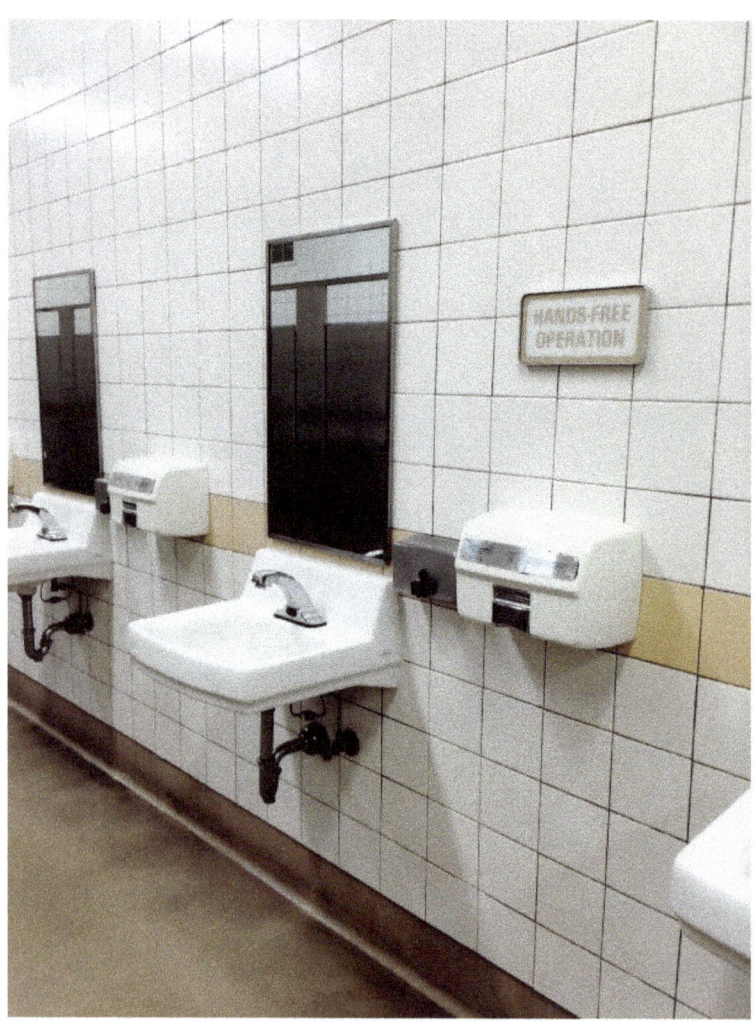

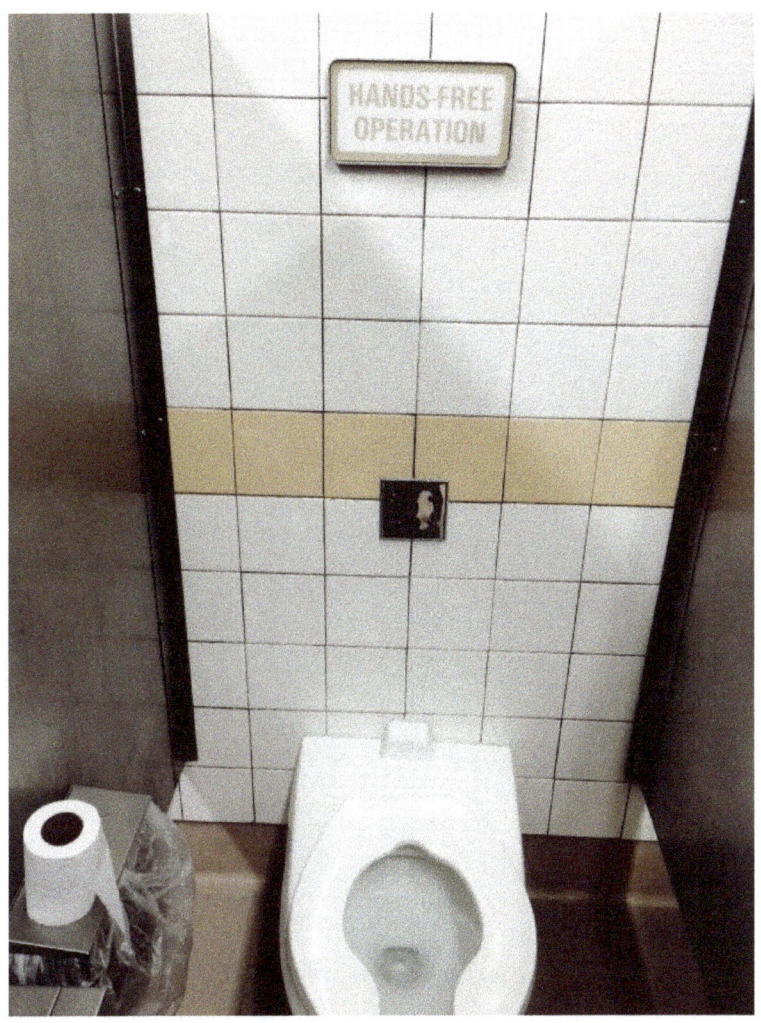

I can't tell you how many times I have made the approach to squat and got splashed because it was an autoflush and I didn't know. The landing pattern is much swifter when it's an autoflush; it has to be.

As if handsanitizer in the toilet stall wasn't weird enough at this truck pit stop along I-75, the gap at the bottom of the door so large one could practically crawl through made this otherwise posh looking toilet not the place I wanted to hang around in for long.

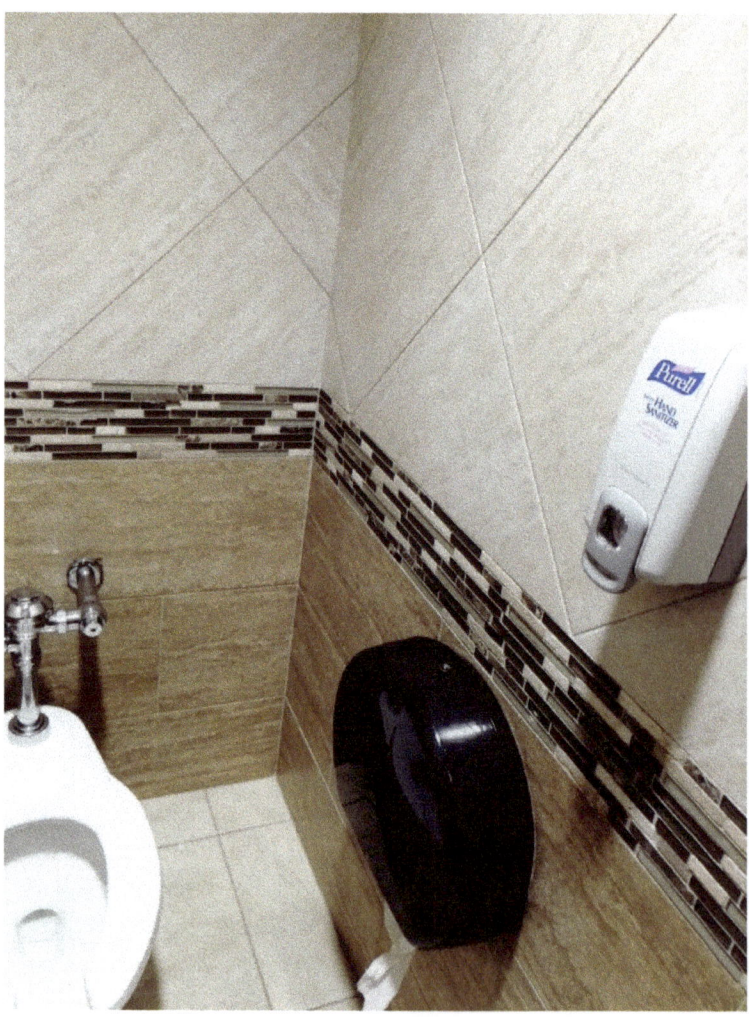

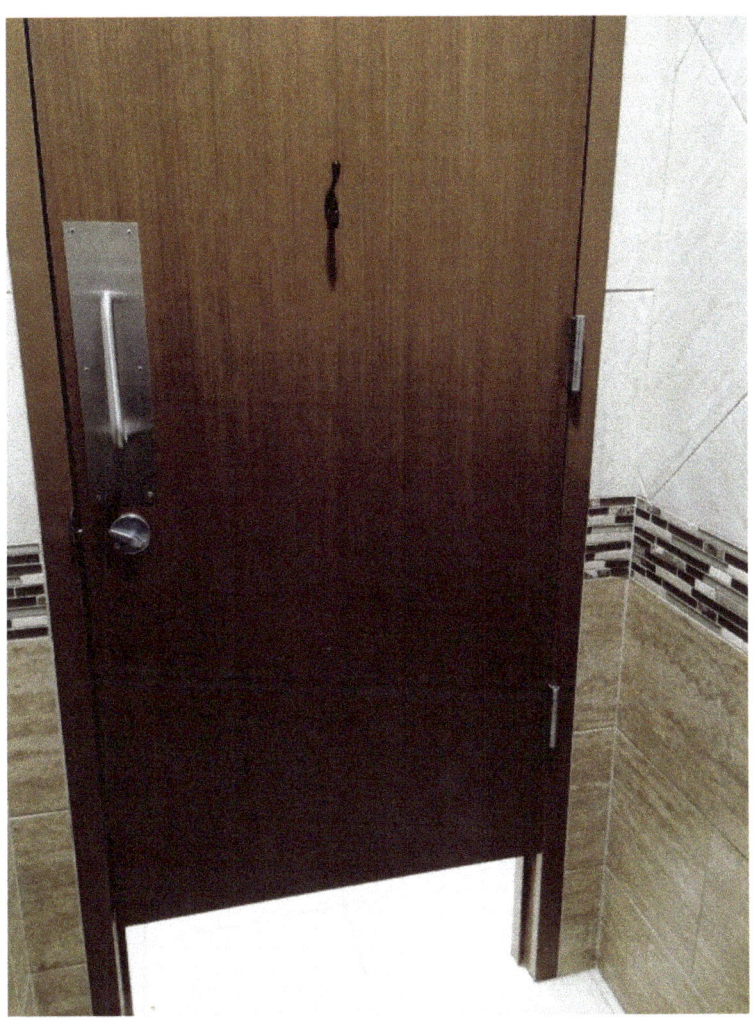

This university bathroom in Ireland solved the problem of idle time with this back-of-the-stall infomercial.

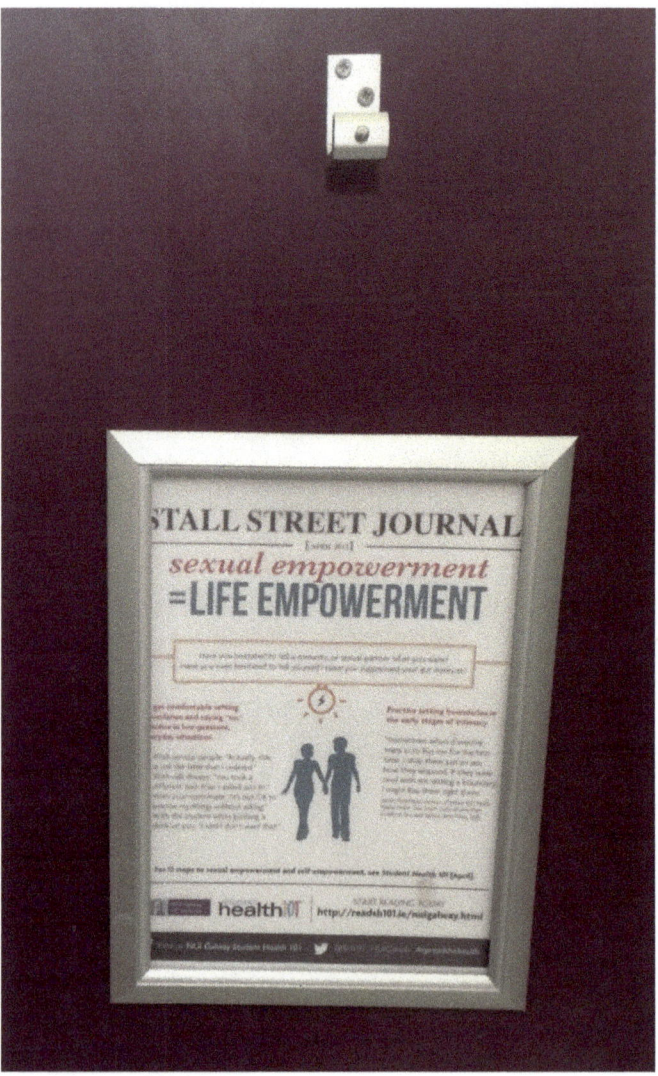

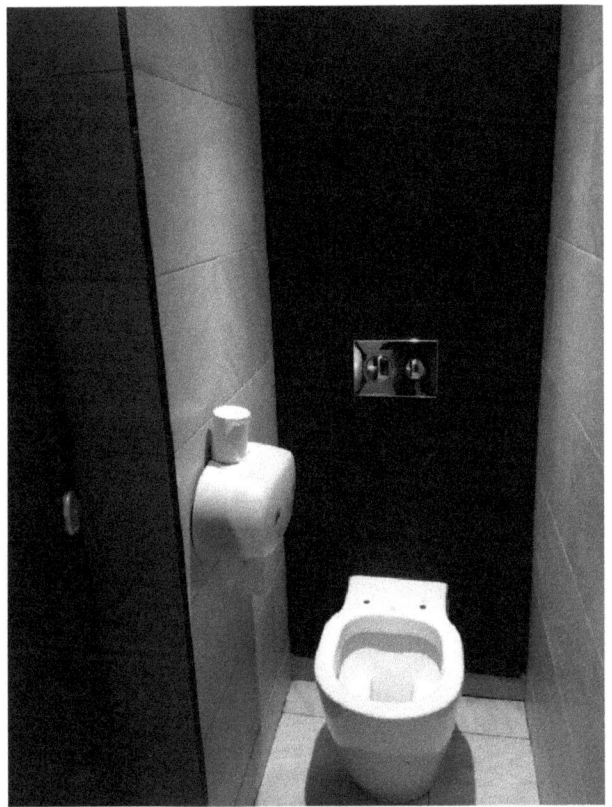

Just in case the extra roll in the dispenser wasn't enough, let's give 'em more on top. But, we'll keep the seat. Here we have a toilet designed to help ladies practice hovering.

This single seater at a fast food place could have easily
been outfitted with two or three stalls.

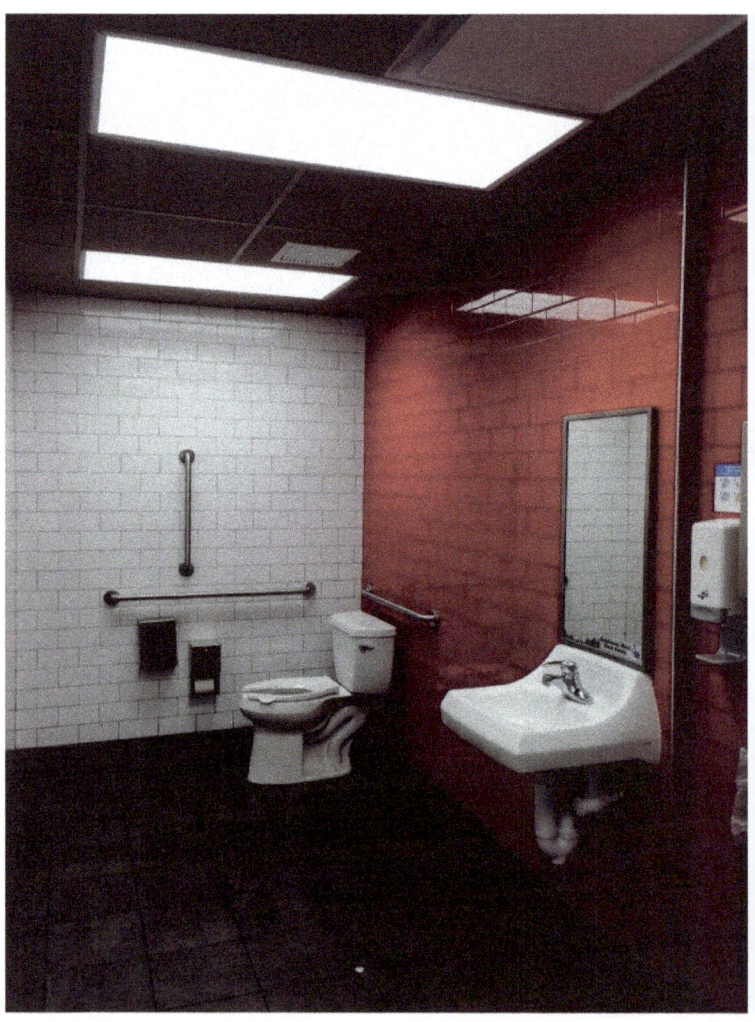

Sure was nice to have all that room to....dance!

It wasn't so much the size of this stall in this fast food restaurant that begged me to snap a picture, and believe me it was quite roomy.

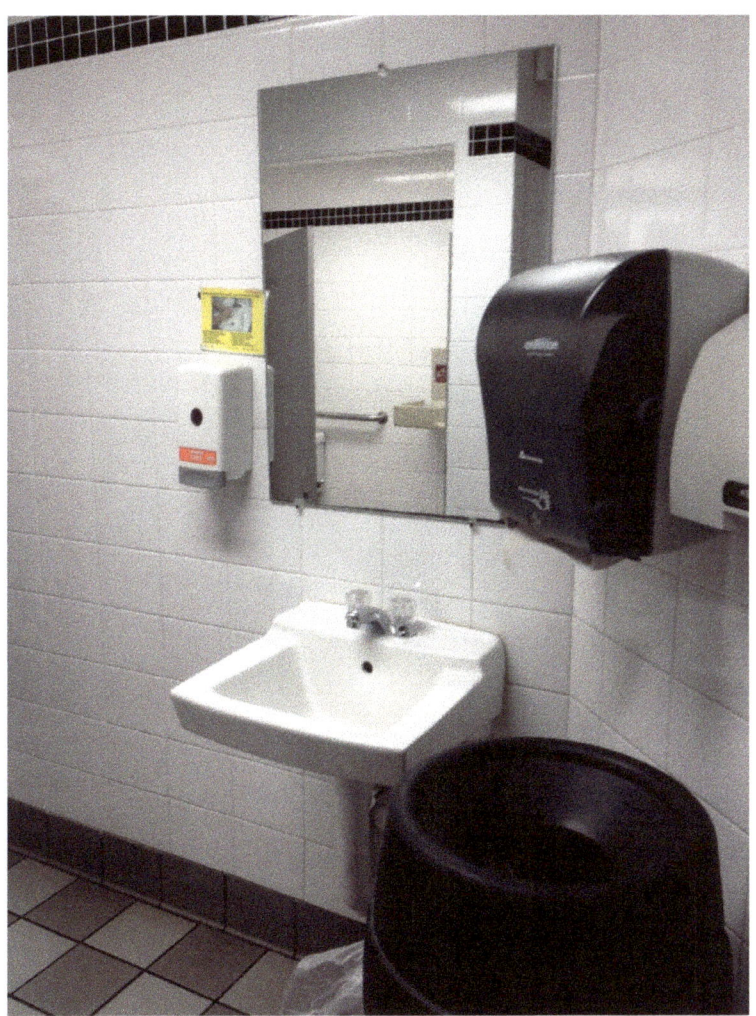

It was the dispenser on the wall!

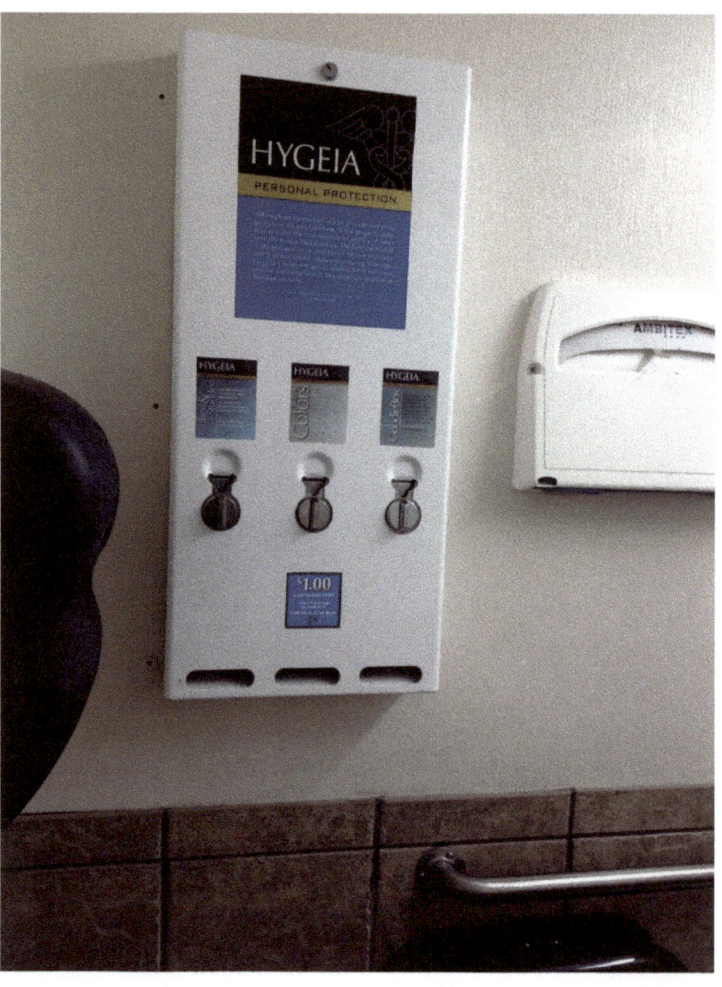

Those machines are fairly common, but inside an individual stall…with a baby changing table?? "Use this machine to stop having to do that," I felt like the proprietors were saying.

This machine was in one of the posh toilets I visited in Ireland.

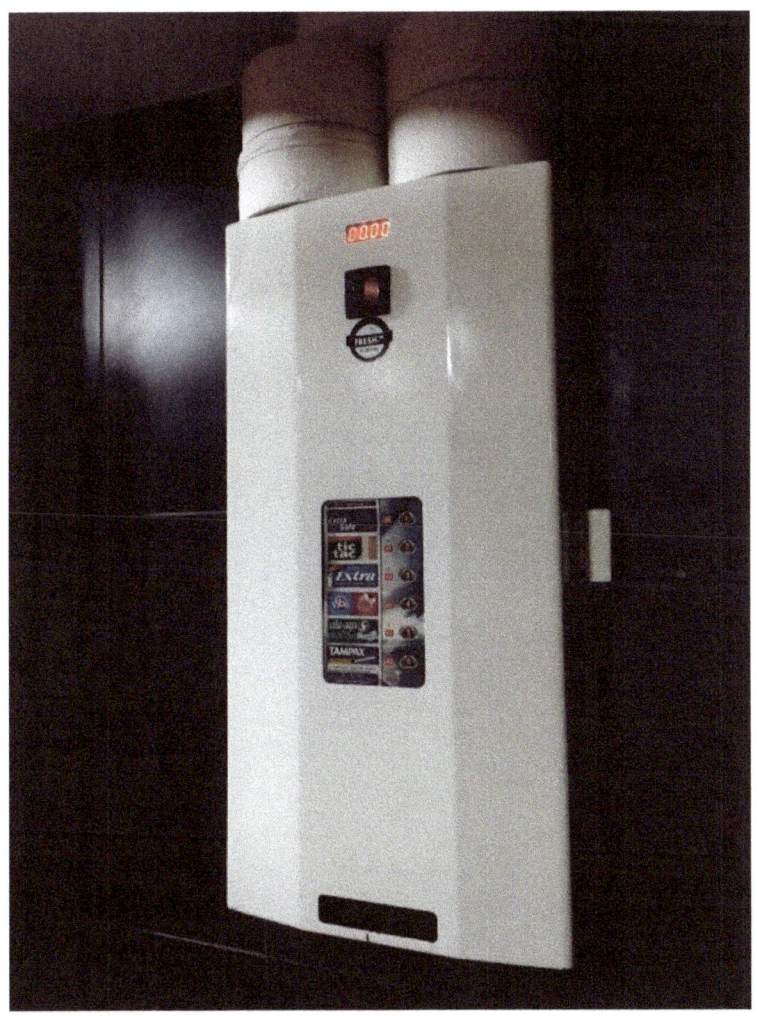

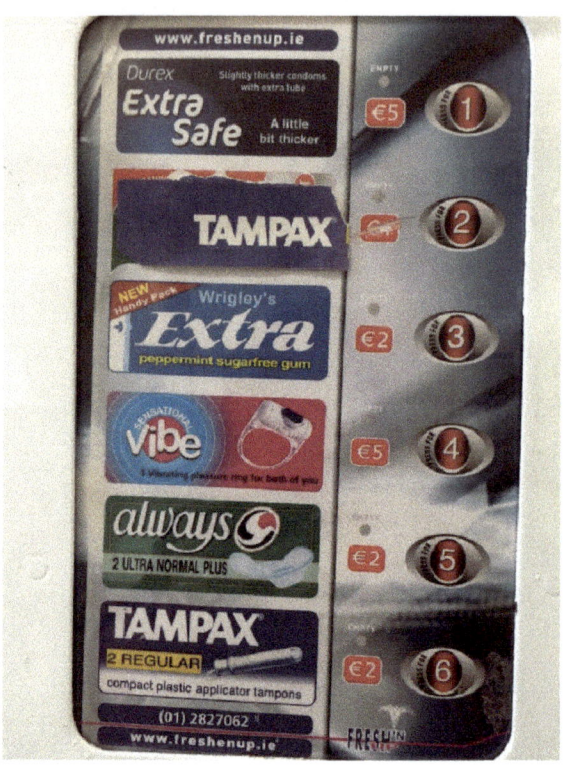

They must want their lady patrons to be prepared for every situation, including a night alone.

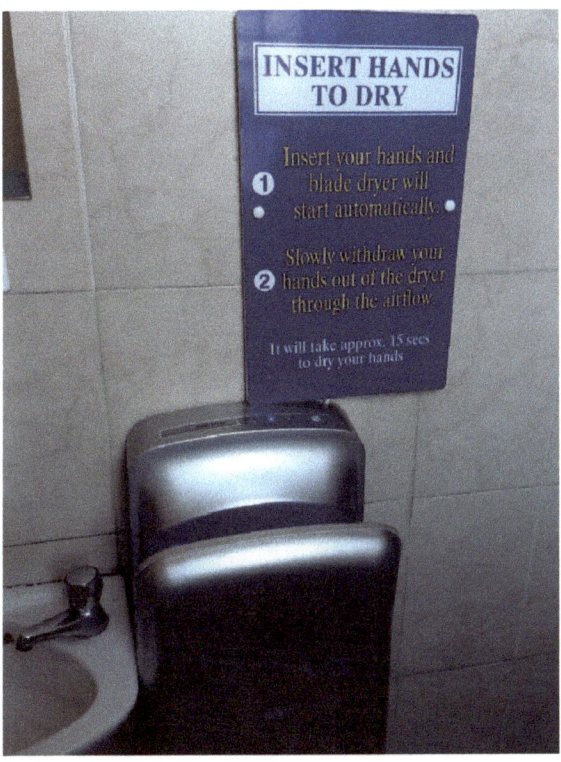

INSERT HANDS
TO DRY

1. Insert your hands and blade dryer will start automatically.

2. Slowly withdraw your hands out of the dryer through the airflow.

It will take approx. 15 secs to dry your hands

Cleanliness is next to godliness and this hand dryer in a church bathroom will certainly blow away any dirt the soap left behind, especially if you leave your hands in it for the recommended 15 seconds.

No, that's not an extra large roll of toilet paper or a roll of paper towels, it's a back rest cushion!

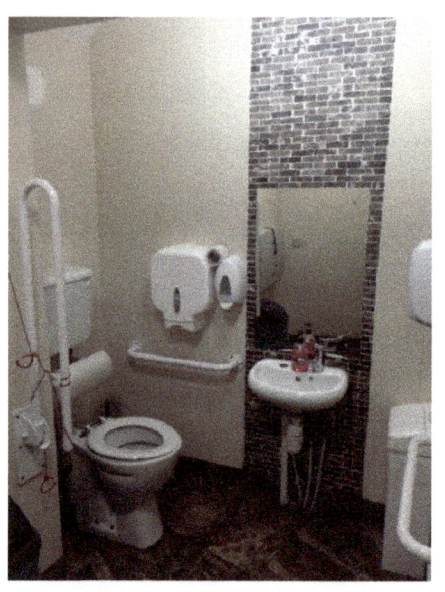

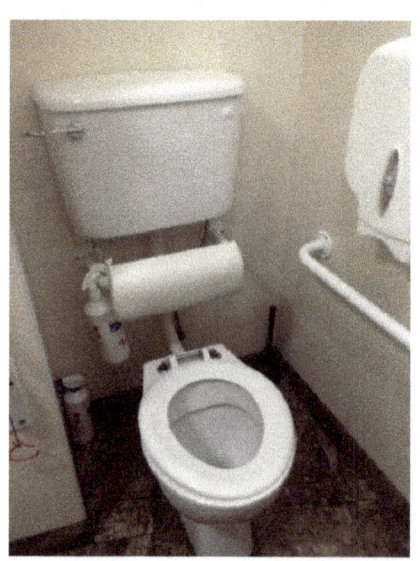

Even in posh professor potties…

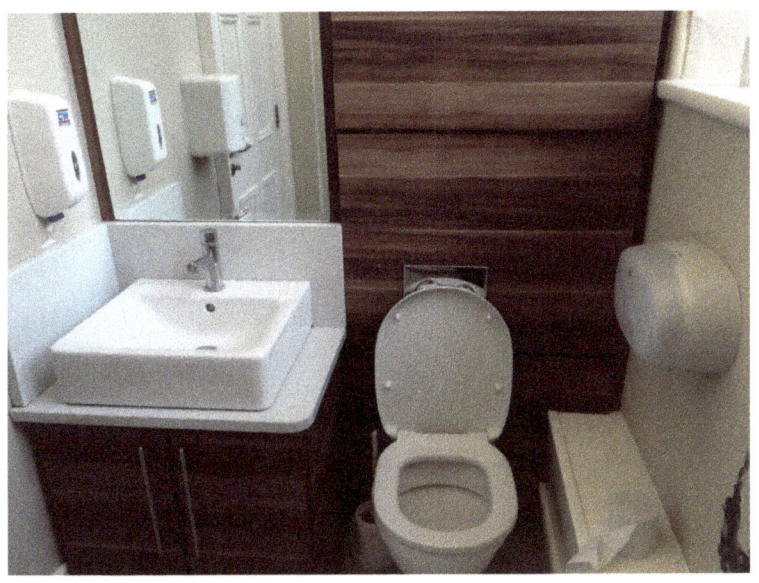

…we mustn't forget that extra roll!

Just be sure you have plenty of time to go so you can figure out the lock. It may say turn twice to lock, but didn't say how many times nor in which direction to turn for unlocking! I nearly missed my field trip bus trying to get out!!

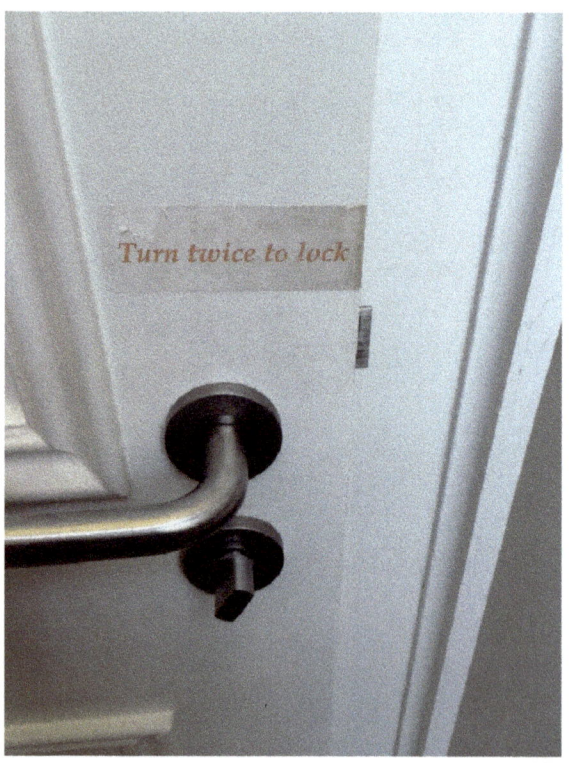

This is the teachers' loo at an Irish all boys secondary academy.

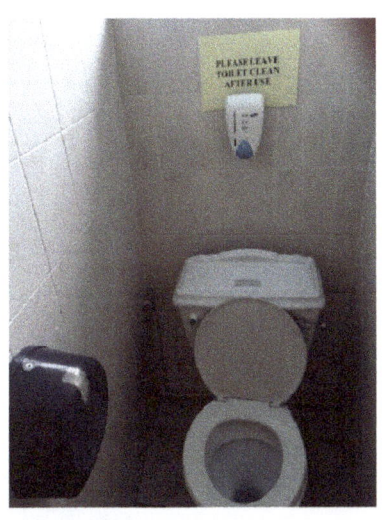

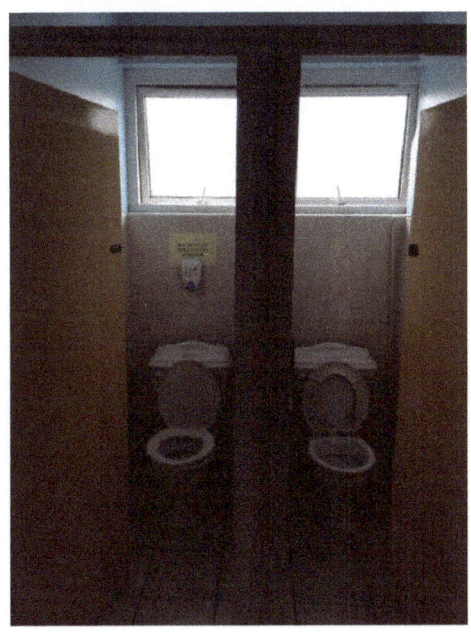

Adults have to be told to tidy up after themselves? Even in Ireland? Funny how only one stall had that requirement.

Teachers all around the world are overworked, even when going for a wee it seems. They can't be left to just simply flush, they are asked to also save water, costing them precious minutes between classes that they don't have.

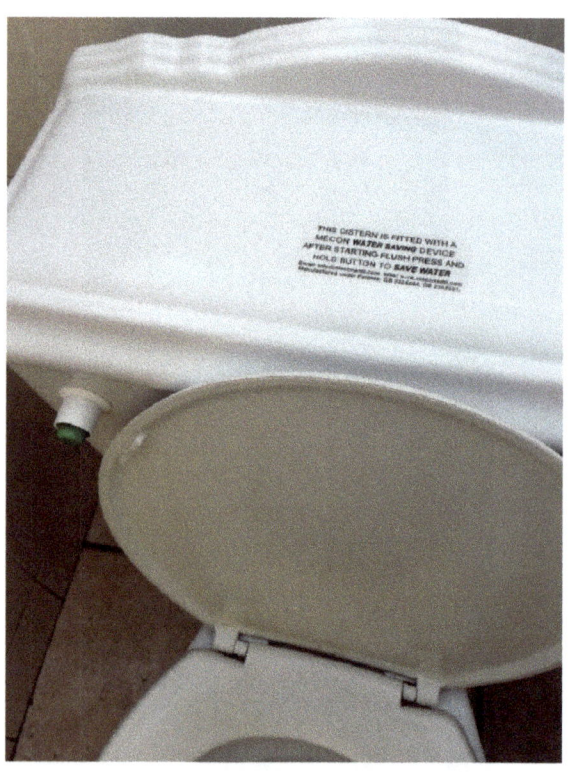

On the last day of our trip to Ireland, my son and I woke very early and grabbed a taxi that would take us to the bus depot to catch the bus that would get us to the nearest airport, more than two hours away, for a 9:00 A.M. flight back home.

By the time we had made it through customs and security and to our departing gate, mother nature, who had previously been patiently waiting, decided I urgently needed to go. No problem, we had passed the restrooms along the way so I knew they were close by. After depositing our carry-ons, I made a beeline for the ladies'.

The first stall was occupied, the second strangely had the seat left up, so I moved on to the third stall. When my yellow tinted eyesight cleared, I got up and turned to flush. But in doing so I felt as if I was giving the wall a proctology exam. It made me think of those who prefer to flush with their feet. If they tried it here, surely they'd jam a toe or worse. I was going to take a picture, but for some reason decided not to.

Bad choice. I think I could have used those extra seconds.

When I emerged from the stall, there in front of me, standing at the sink and staring pale faced into the mirror was a stately looking Irish gentleman. "Oh dear, have I gone in the wrong one?" he gasped.

I stood frozen for a second, then looked around. "No, it was me," I barely whispered before running from there as quickly as my short legs, and what little dignity I had left, would allow.

I really wished I could have been brave enough to go back and take a picture, then you would see how easy it was for me to have not recognized straight away that I was in the wrong restroom. Instead you will need to use your imagination as you view these next few pictures of Irish male facilities. Not at all like the ones in the U.S.

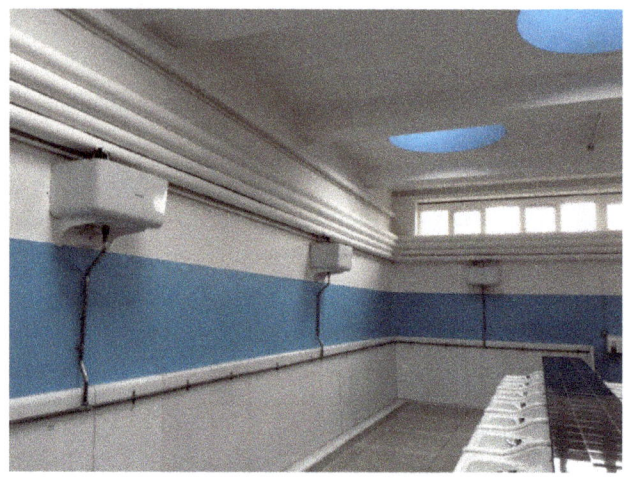

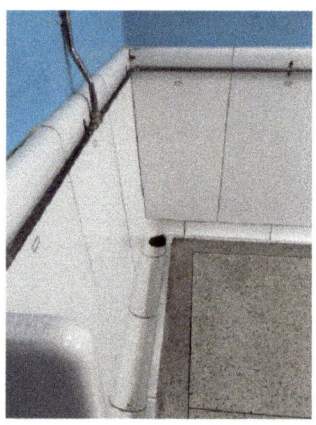

The tanks on the wall hold the flushing water for the "urinal" below. The water flows in a steady light stream down the wall to the shallow trough in the floor and it all washes down a drain located in the bottom of the trough, directly below each tank.

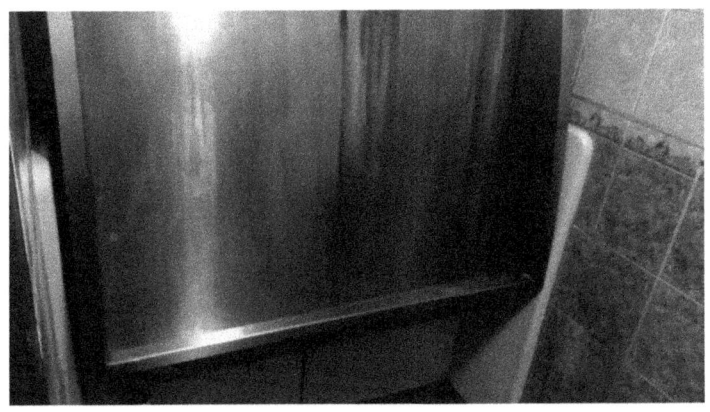

Once he started school, I guess I stopped paying attention to my son's toilet habits. I mean I never knew that throughout his middle and high school years that he refused to relieve himself until he got home. During our trip to Ireland, I learned that this routine had apparently turned into a habitual of avoidance of public restrooms all together. Come to think of it now I don't recall him ever requiring the facilities on any of our outings in the last three years. Oh the irony! On our vacation, walking was our mode of transportation around town. One night after dinner he decided he needed to go and asked that we quickly make our way back to the Bed and Breakfast. This is when his habit came to light and I found myself in a silly argument. So, I threw down the "mom" card and made him go to the toilet. He came back to the table much relieved but with a puzzled look on his face. When he told me about the "urinal" I asked (no, begged, practically nagged) my son to go back and take a picture. He was none too pleased but in the end complied. Men peeing on a wall now makes sense to me. They do it in the public restrooms!

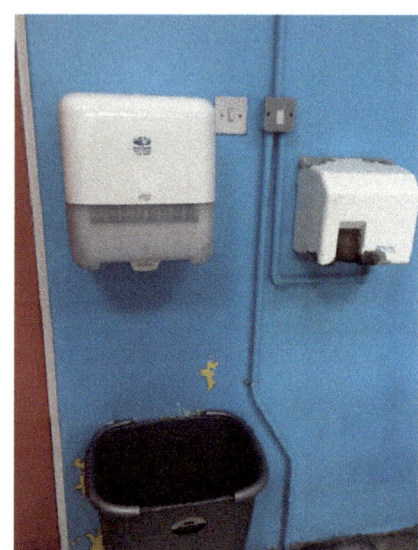

The paper towel dispenser over the trashcan makes much more sense than the dispenser over a radiator. If you can't wipe your hands dry, burn the water off instead.

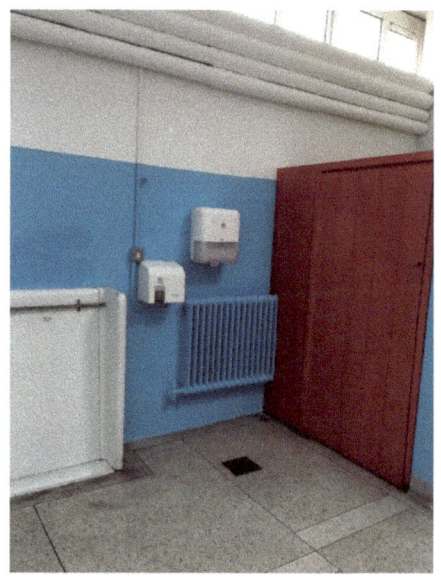

This bathroom looks poised to service a large number of students at one time, maybe two or three classes at a shot. But why then, are there only five soap dispensers? The one tiny mirror high on the wall certainly indicates no female presence was ever planned to be here.

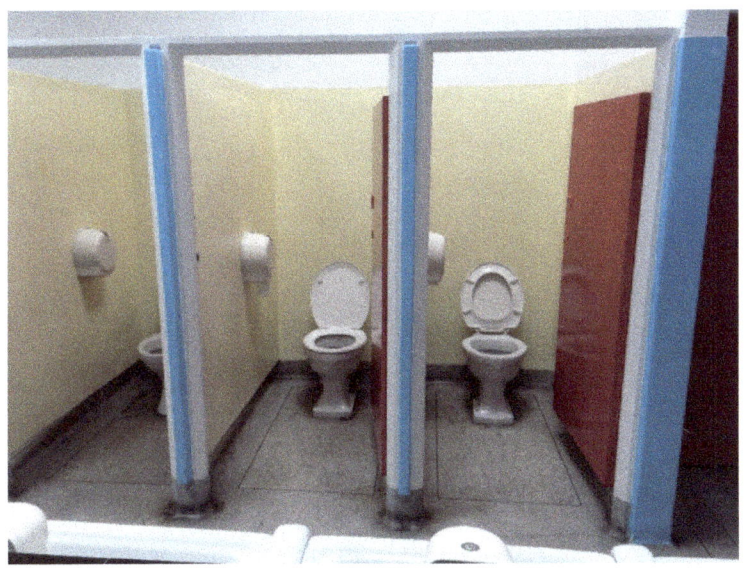

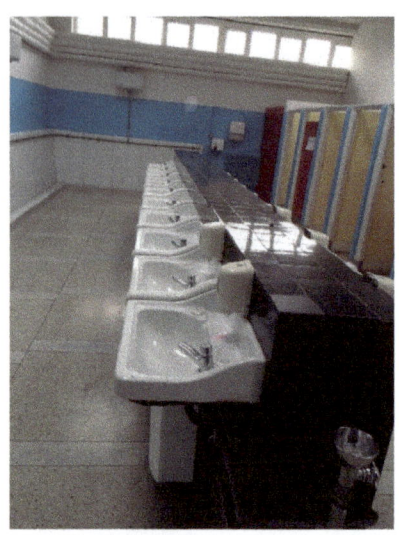

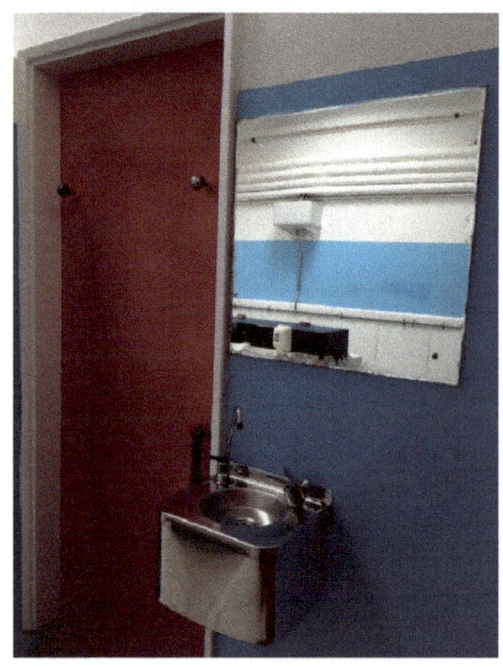

The 'guest' toilet at the front entrance to St. Mary's all boys secondary school looked so very posh, and inviting, until one looked up. Makes you wonder how effectively they kept the students out, or if this was the work of grown up kids.

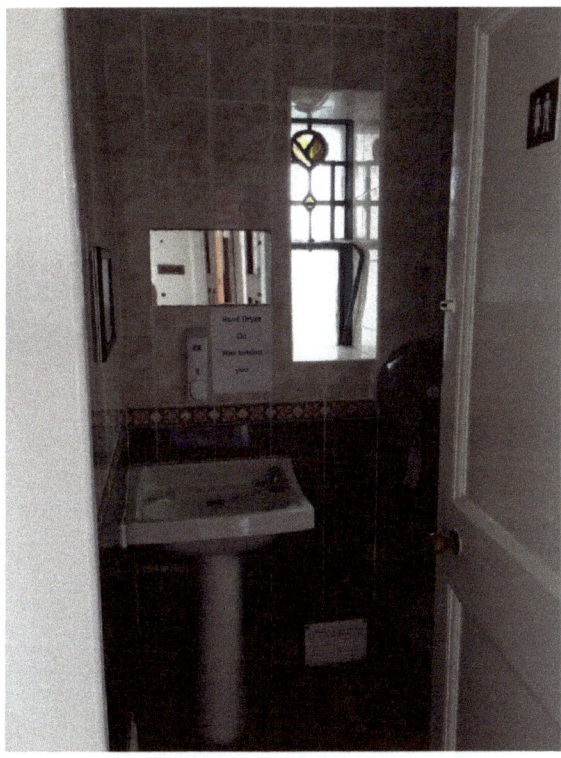

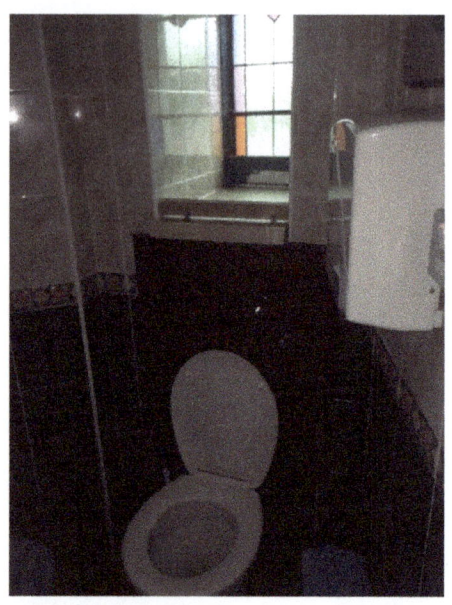

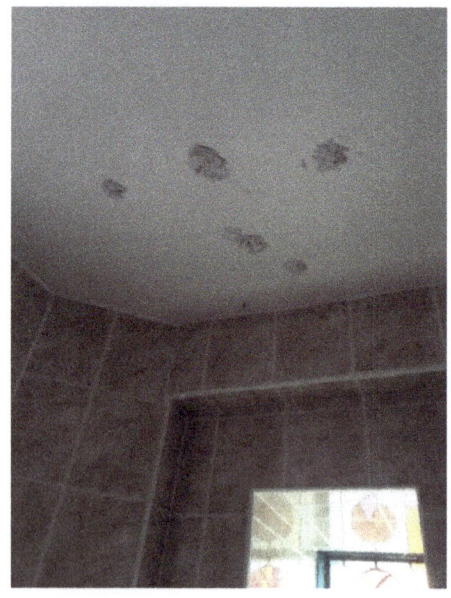

Who doesn't immediately turn around after washing their hands?

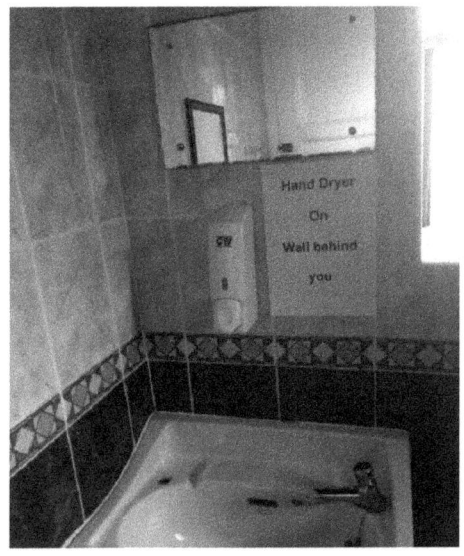

The little box is the switch that turns on and off the current to the adjacent receptacle. The light indicates the juice is flowing.

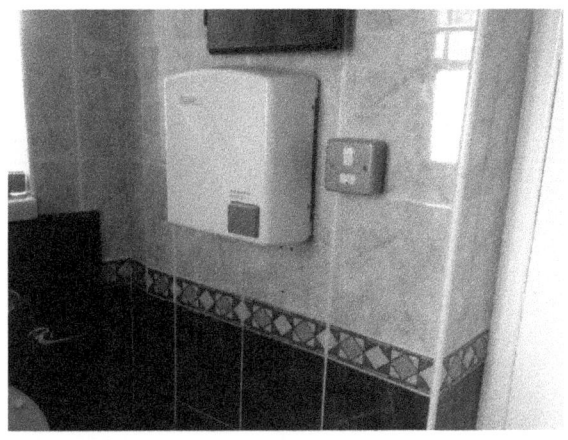

If you have a lock on the bathroom door that clearly lets people know the room is occupied, and it's a one-seater, why, then, do you need a stall door with a lock?

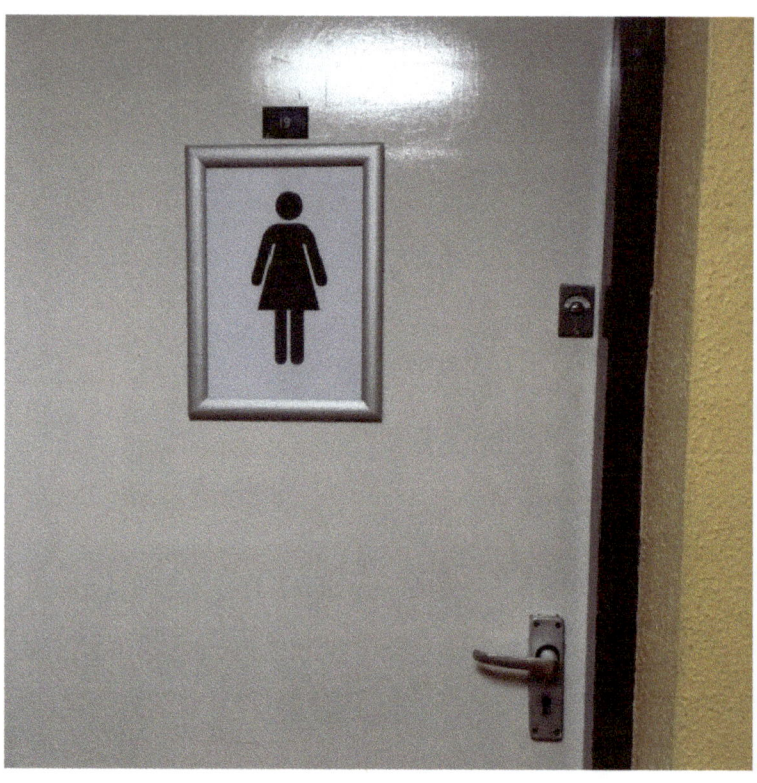

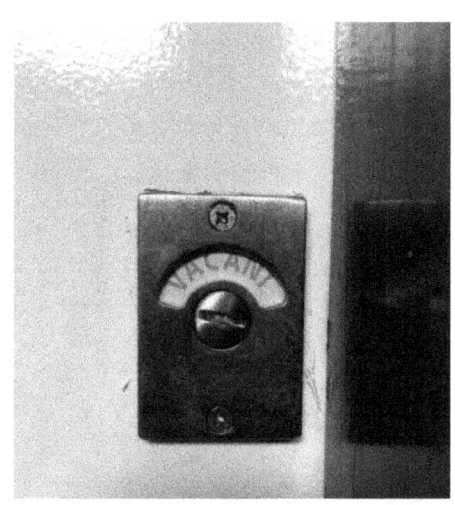

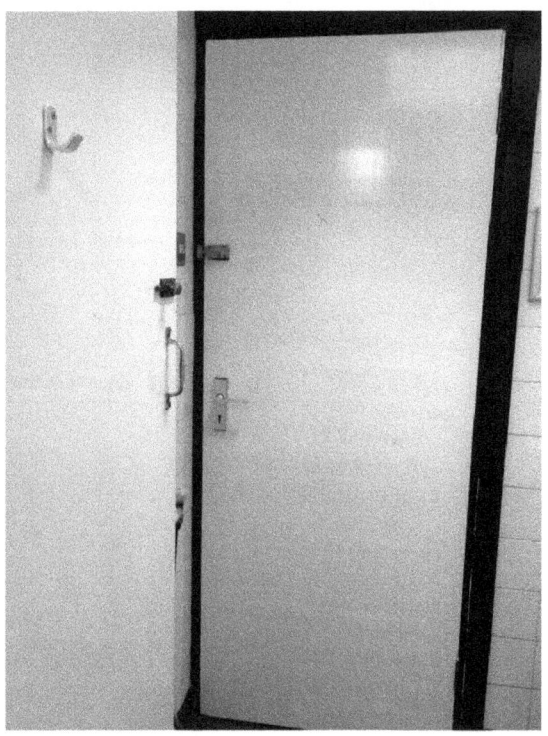

Do women really go to the bathroom in pairs….at school?
Is this chair for her friend waiting her turn?

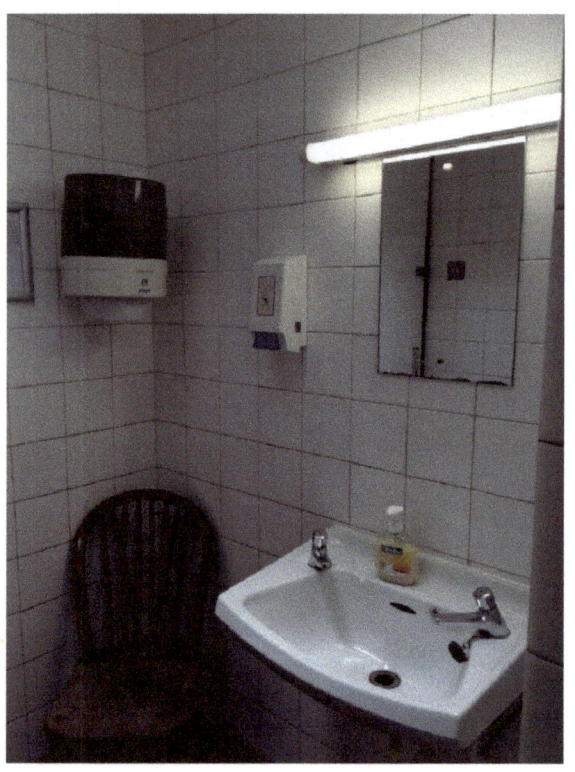

At Klymore Abbey you clearly are not to even think about drinking the water.

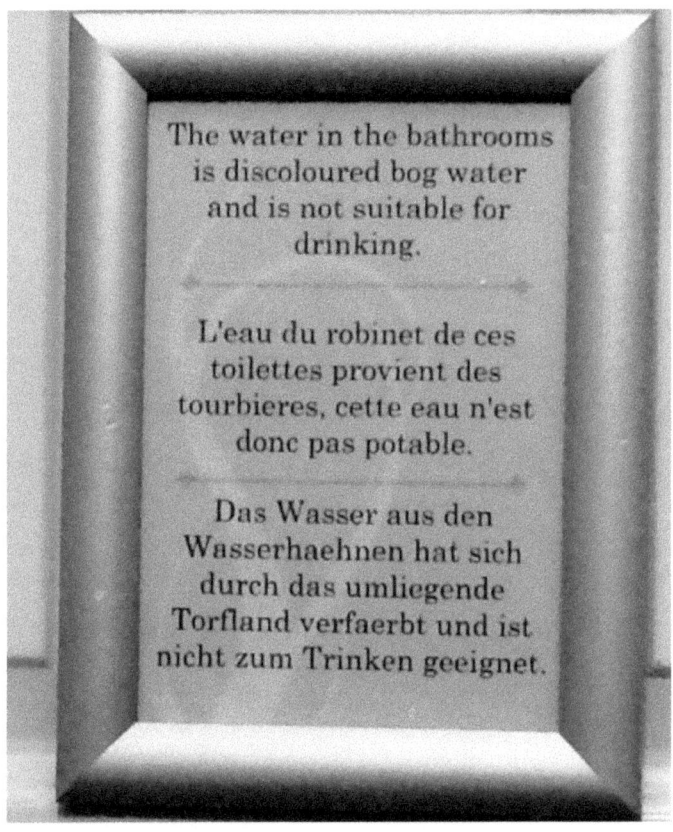

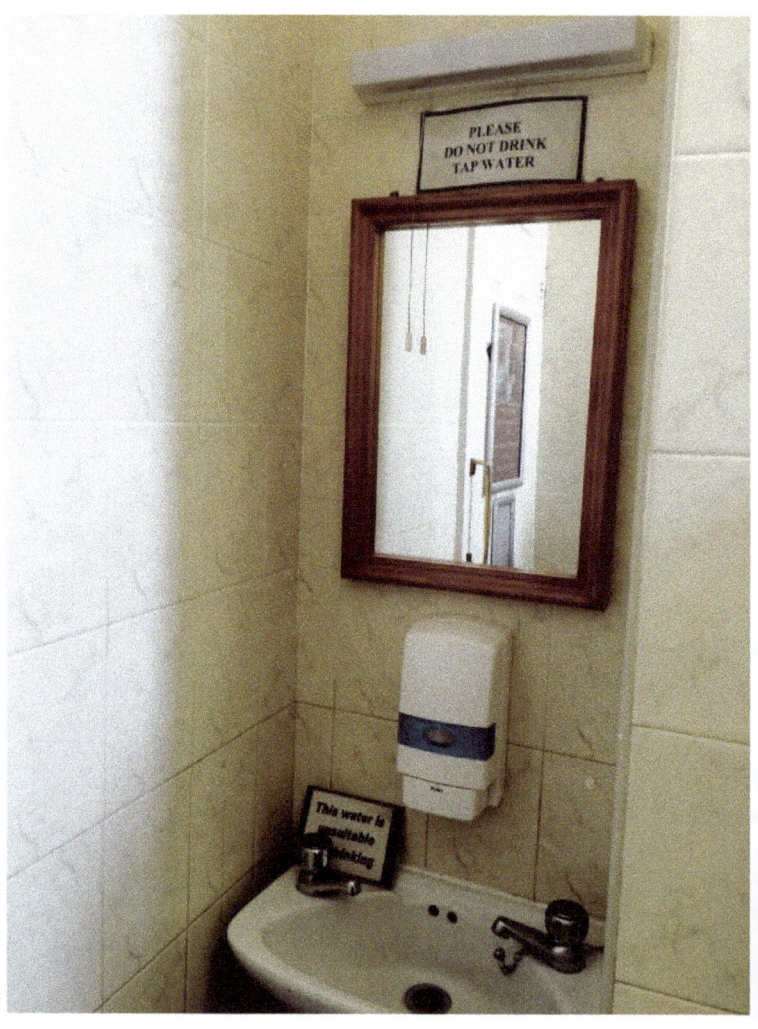

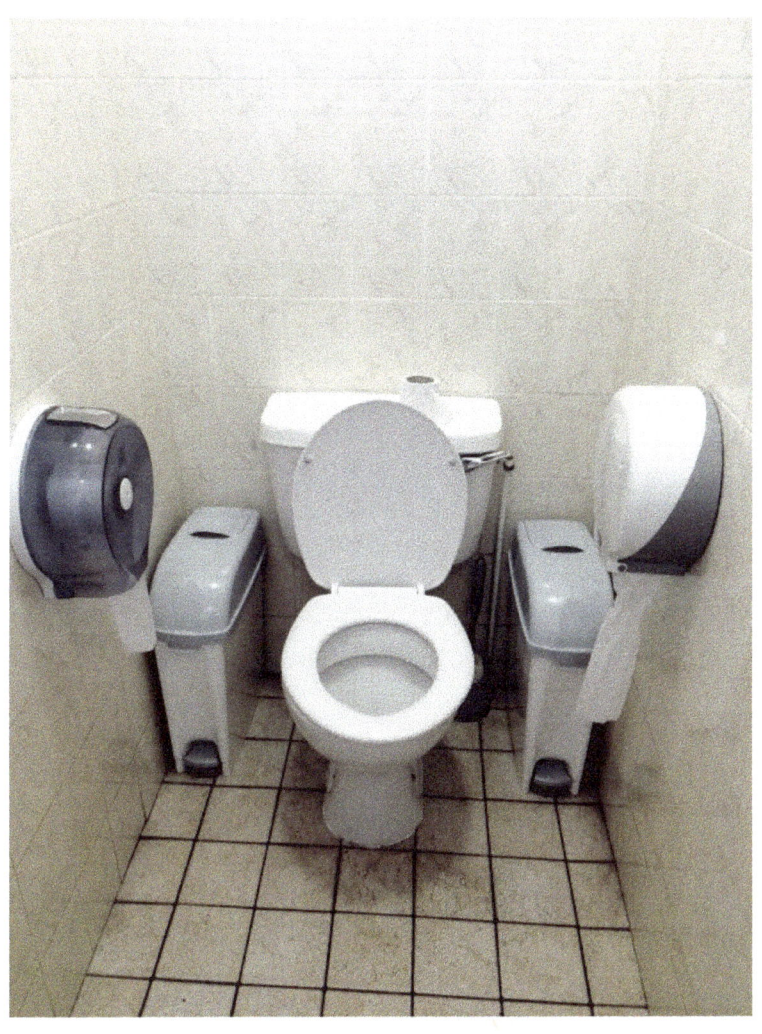

Like lefty/righty scissors,
now we have a lefty/righty toilet.

Student toilets were in the basement of the main building at the National University of Ireland at Galway.

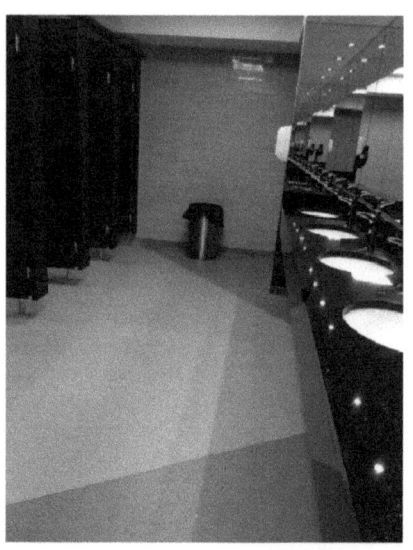

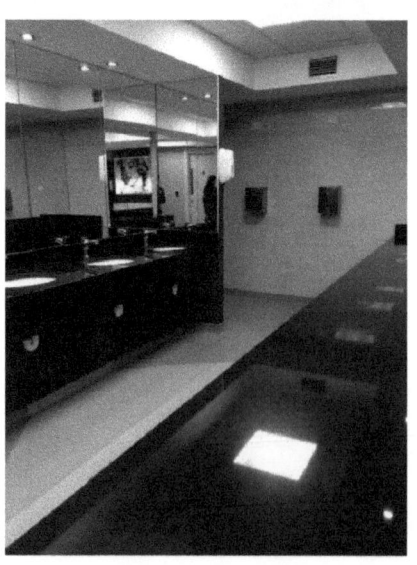

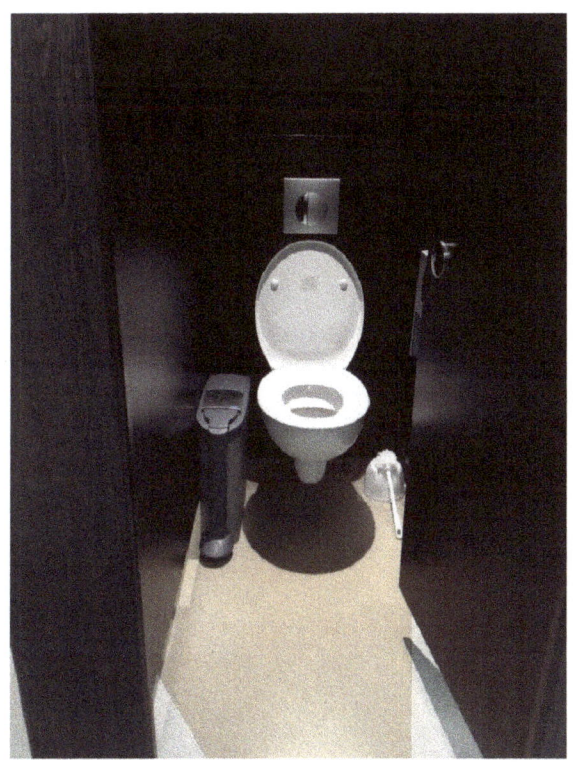

You may have had to climb down some scary steps, but the posh loo at the bottom was well worth the trip. Just ask Marilyn.

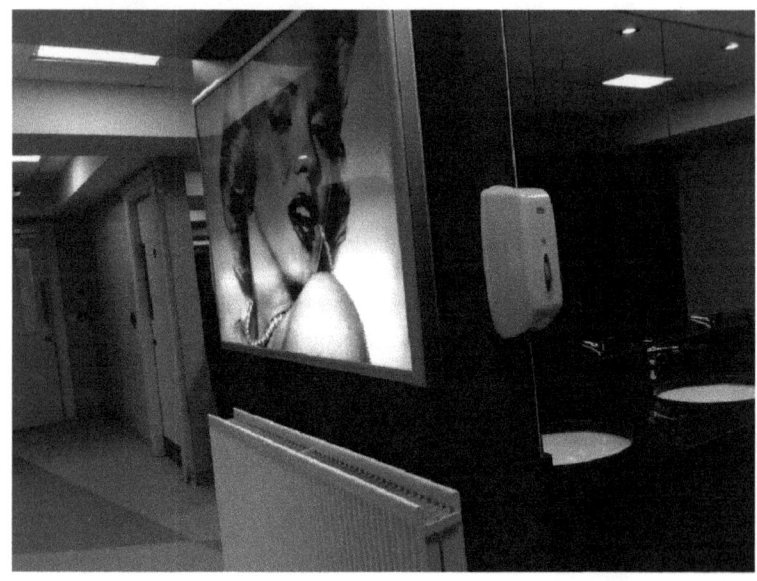

* * *

It seems the best place for truly posh toilets in Ireland is in the basement. This was the fanciest toilet I had been to in a long time, but it was quite a quest to get there. I was going down such long hallways that led so far back into the building, away from the main dining area, and down so many stairs that I thought I was going to need to start leaving breadcrumbs to find my way back.

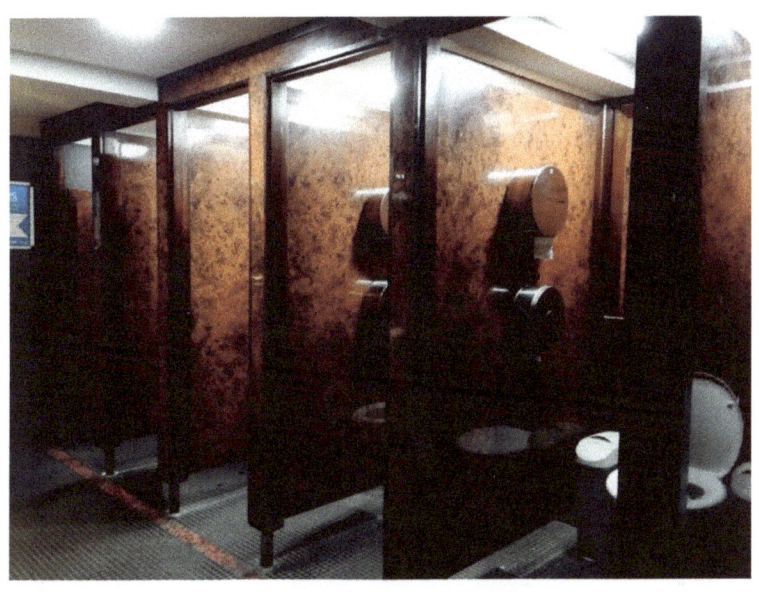

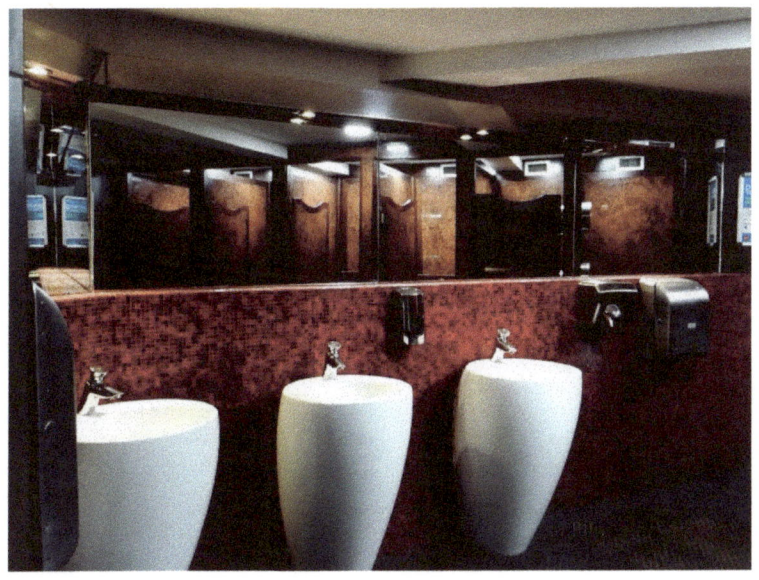

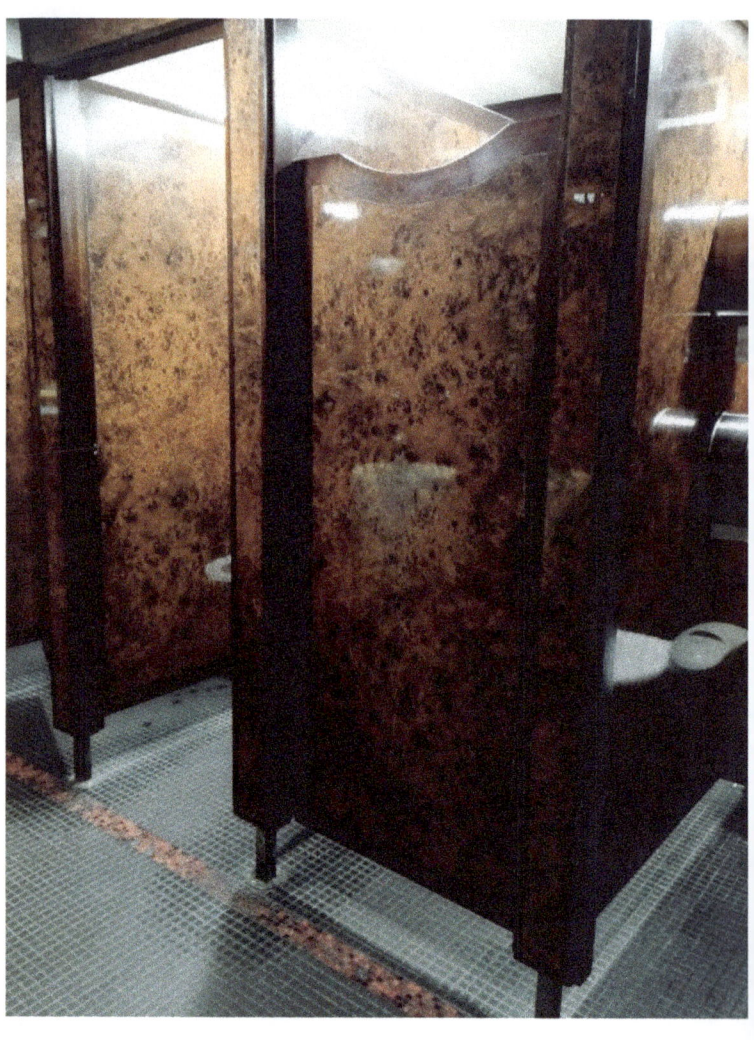

Still one must wonder, how long of a reach these people expect their customers to have to have placed the toilet paper dispenser so far up the wall.

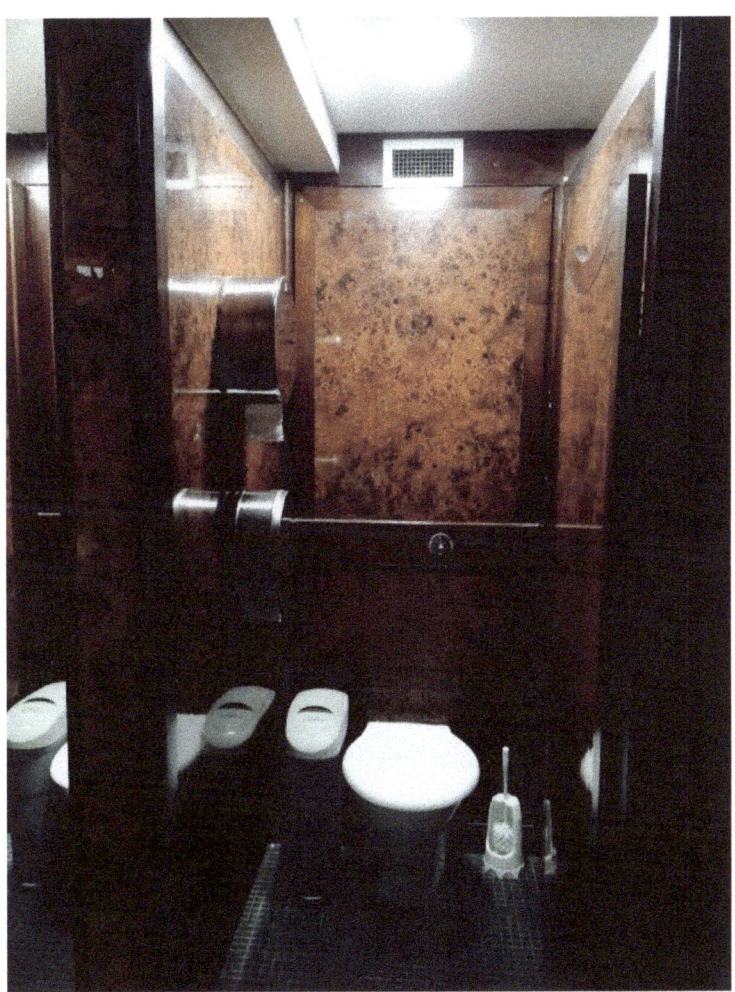

Luckily, for vertically challenged people like myself, there was a nearer option.

I was absolutely blown away by the power of the flush in these toilets, I had to know how this was possible.

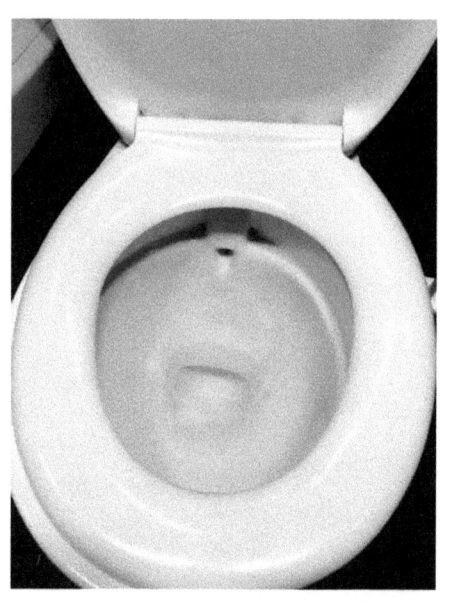

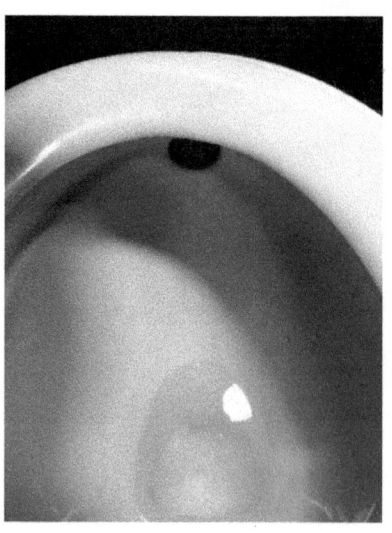

It's amazing to see local establishments using local materials to build. Even more amazing when those materials are as ornate as this Connemara marble from Galway County, Ireland.

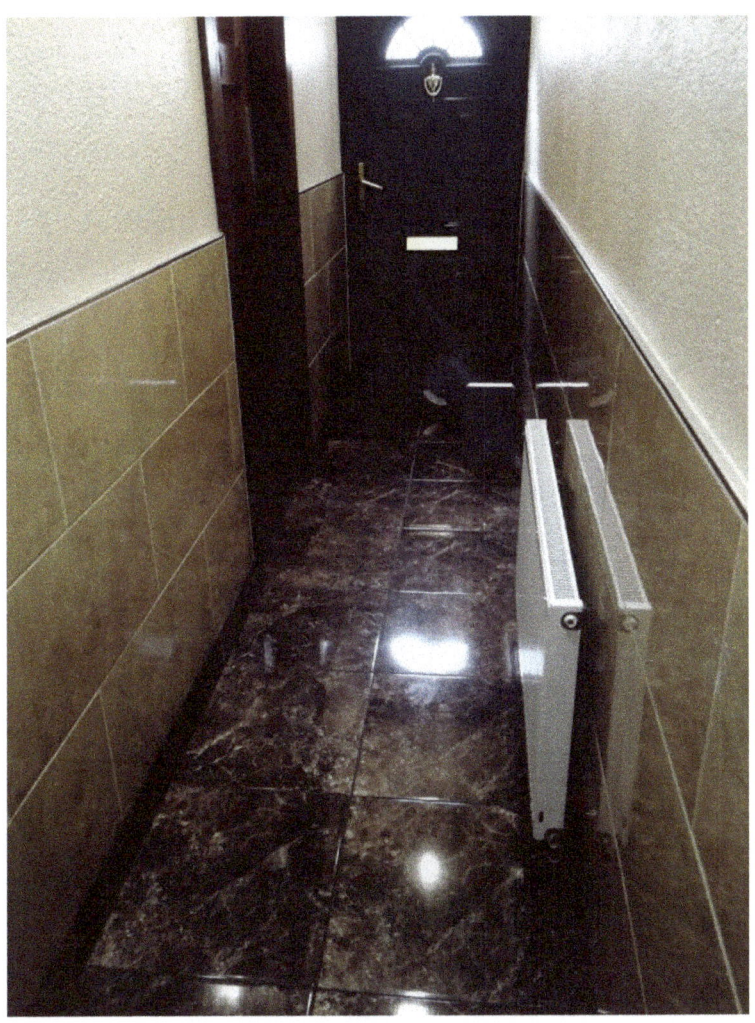

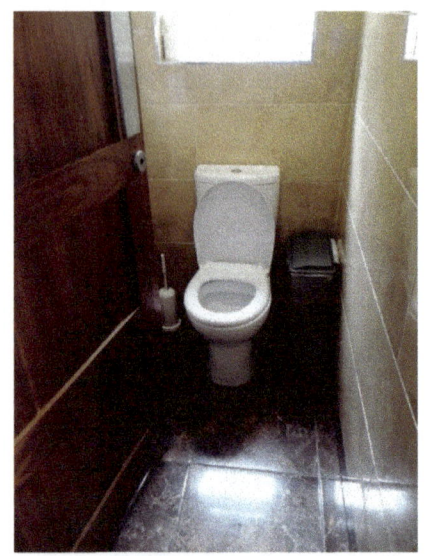

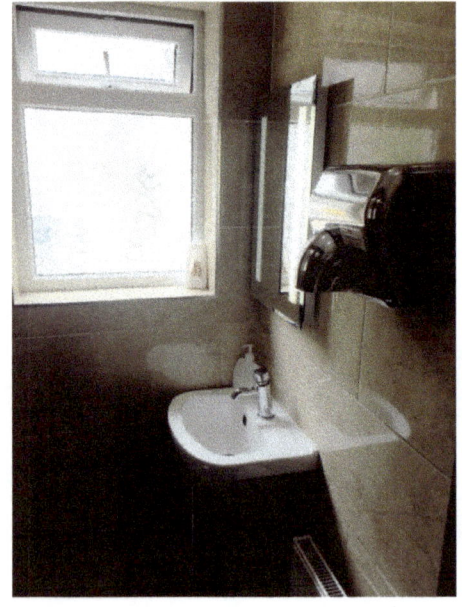

Sinks that don't look like sinks.

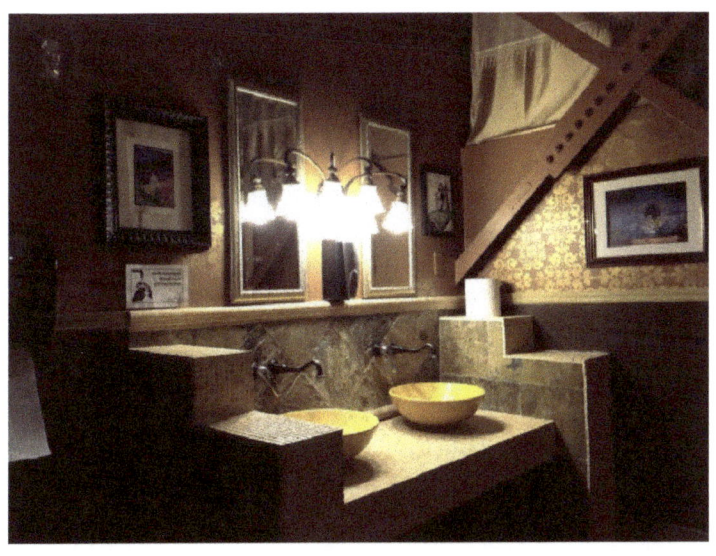

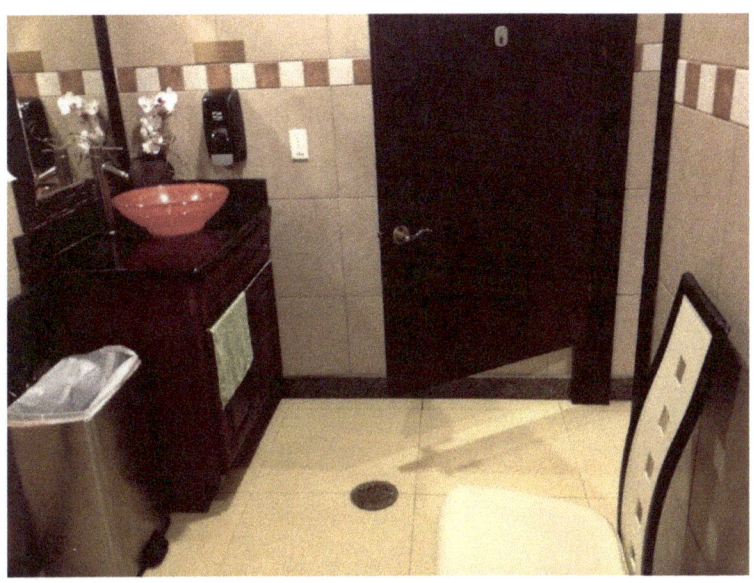

So that you never lose track of the amount of time you occupy the throne, as so many of us do when out in public, this establishment has given you a convenient clock on the back of the door rather than a hook for your purse.

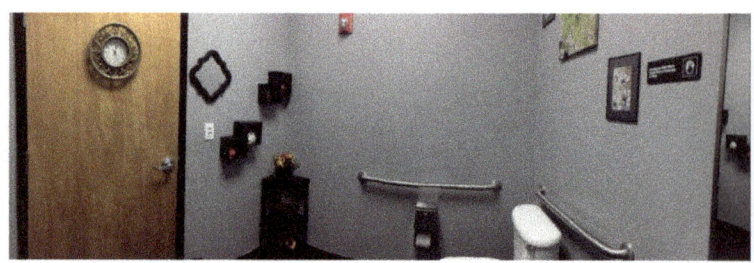

* * *

The scariest experience of my life while answering nature's call was had in a pay toilet in the heart of Eyre Square. You would have thought sitting on the throne in the middle of the night in a tiny room barely wide enough for a commode on the bottom floor of a three level house during an earthquake would have topped that list. But no, those walls that swayed like curtains in a gale gust had nothing on this timed, self cleaning, pay toilet in Ireland. It trumped anything I ever experienced while having a wee in Japan.

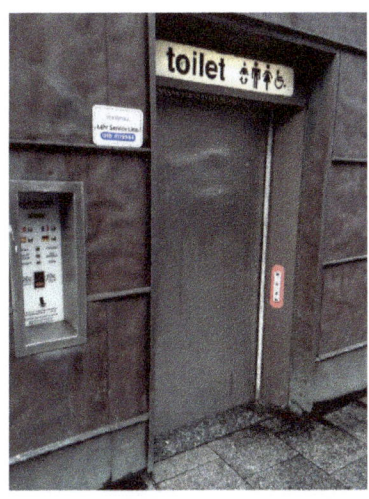

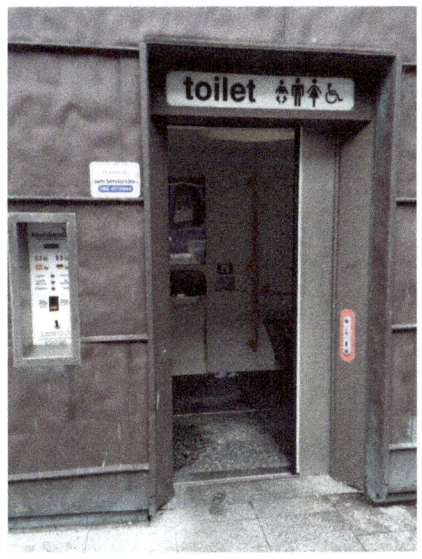

The panel informed you whether the toilet was vacant, occupied or out of order, and collected your 20 cent coin.

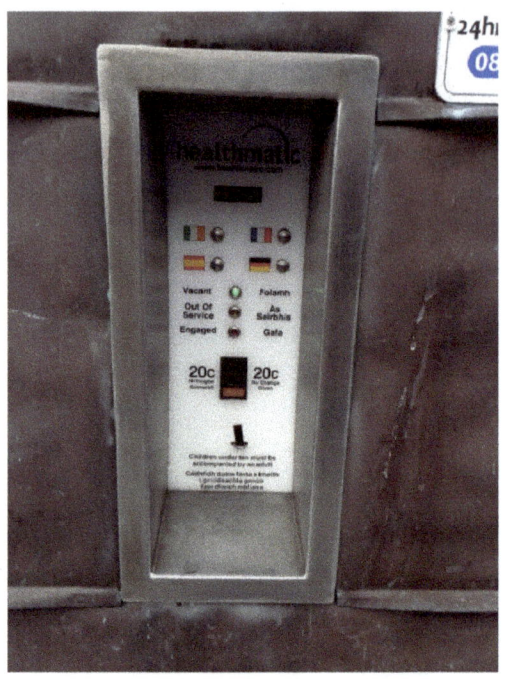

No change was given, it had to be that exact coin or nothing. The LCD display only said self-cleaning toilet. I imagine it would in the appropriate language also when you pressed one of the flag buttons.

* * *

There was good reason for the bright yellow bars everywhere for you to hold onto as you navigated the slippery floor (see next page). The puddles of water all over the floor should have been my first clue to be afraid, very afraid. But, because of my floating eyeballs I decided to venture forth. I had paid my 20 cents so I was going to use it.

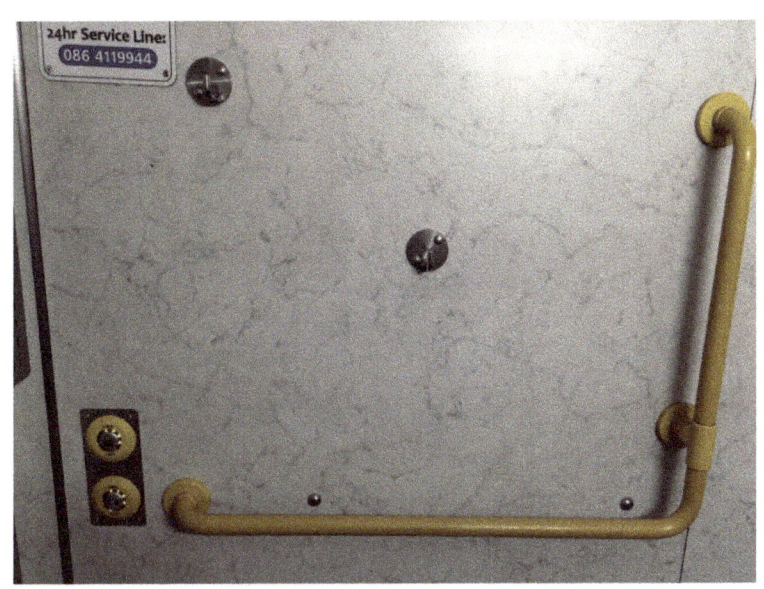

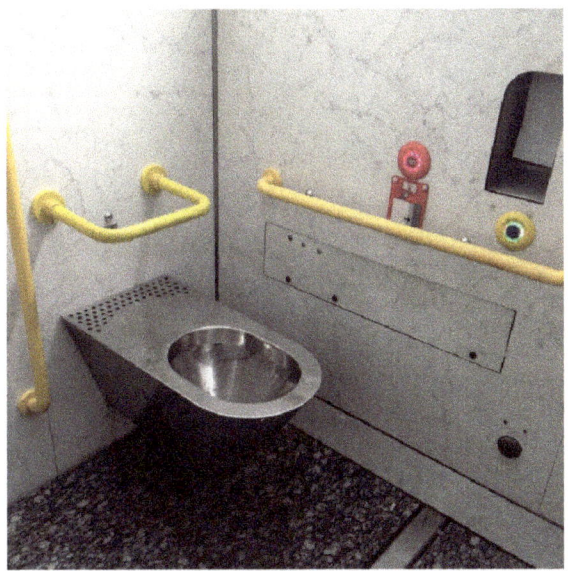

Certainly the place to perfect that hovering technique.

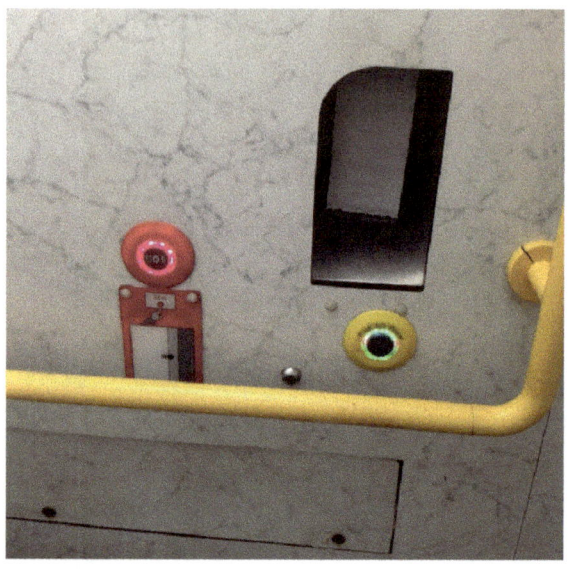

I couldn't understand at the time why you would need to push the button for toilet paper. Thankfully it was generous enough to give you a small length every time you pushed it, and there seemed to be no limit of pushes. Within handy reach of the toilet seat was the emergency button that came with just one drawback. It would immediately fling the door open wide when pushed.

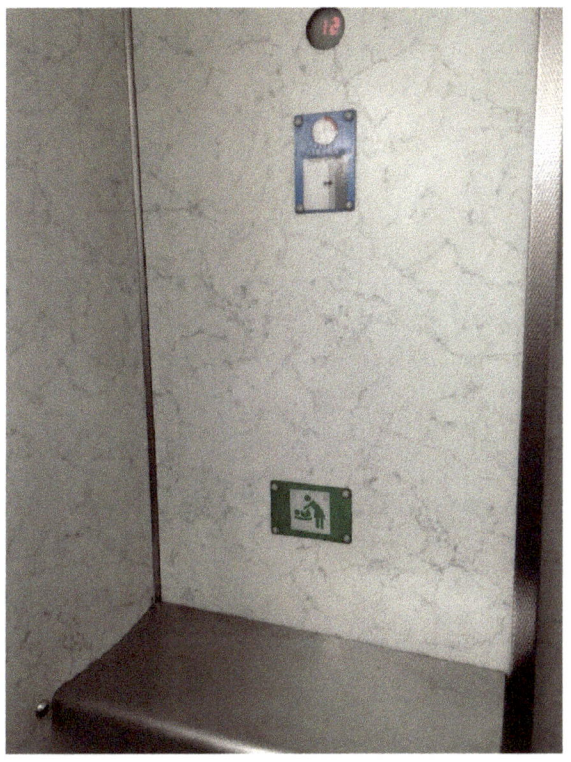

It was kind of them to provide a diaper changing station, however with the 15 minutes allowed one would need to decide a preference for the doors flying open while

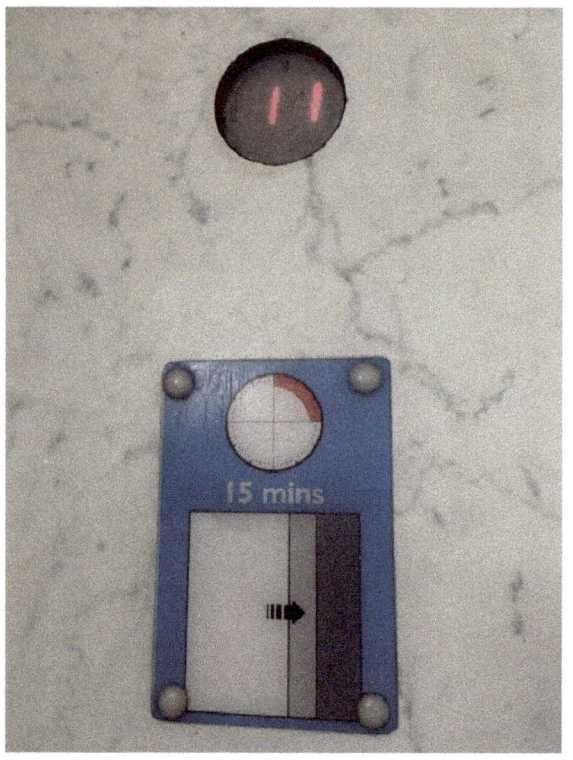

changing baby or while relieving oneself. At the end of that count down the door flies open and the jets spray!

Inserting my hands anywhere in that place was the furthest thing from my mind!

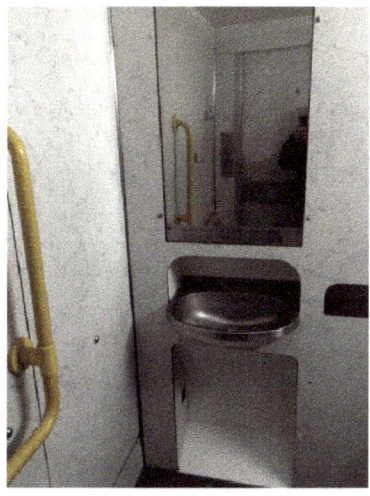

In case you were not stuck working things out, and could be finished early they made a way for you to open the door.

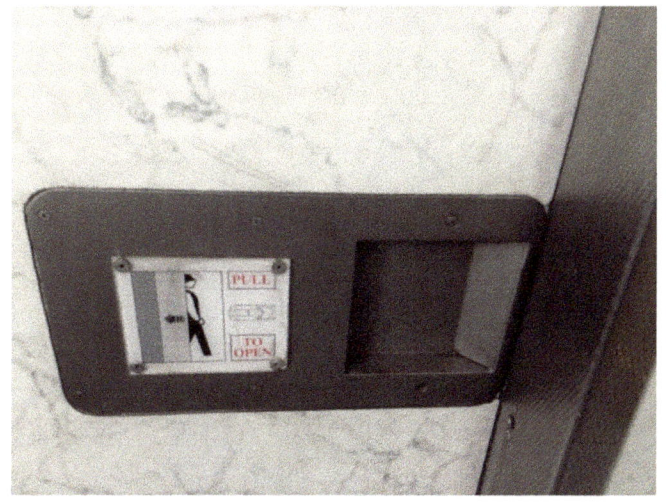

I got out of there as quickly as possible, after taking the pictures of course. When the door closed behind me a gale force wind sound of water jets sprayed the whole place washing anything and everything away.

* * *

This stately façade on a pay toilet across the street from the Galway Cathedral belied the fact that it was just as intimidating as the one I narrowly escaped from in Eyre Square.

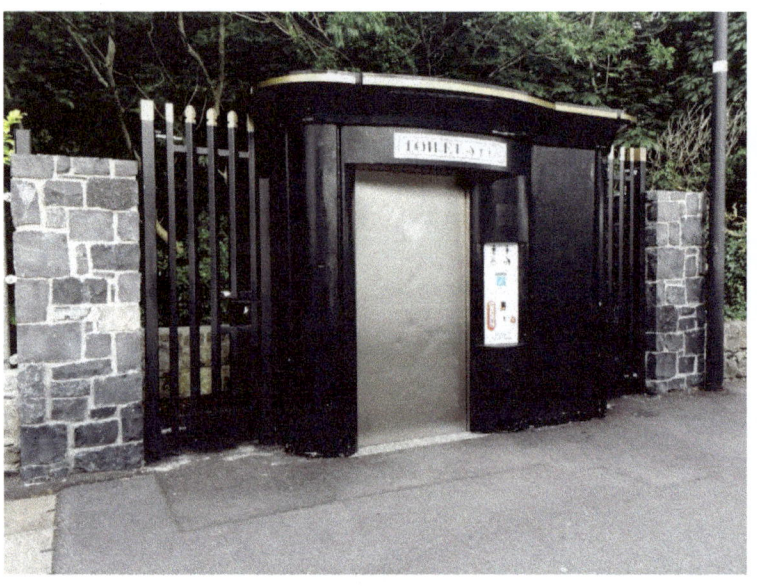

You know it's a friendly town when strangers will happily make change to give you a 20 cent coin outside a pay toilet stall.

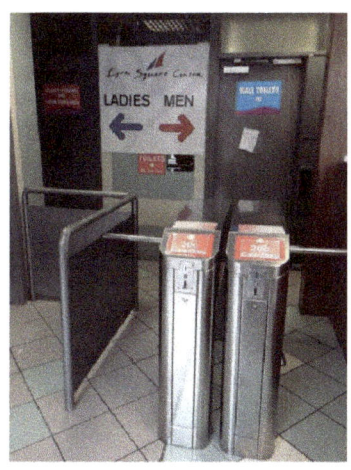

Perhaps this one should have been self cleaning too.

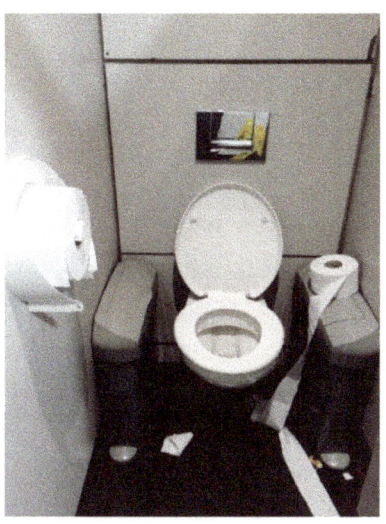

Pay toilets weren't all bad though.

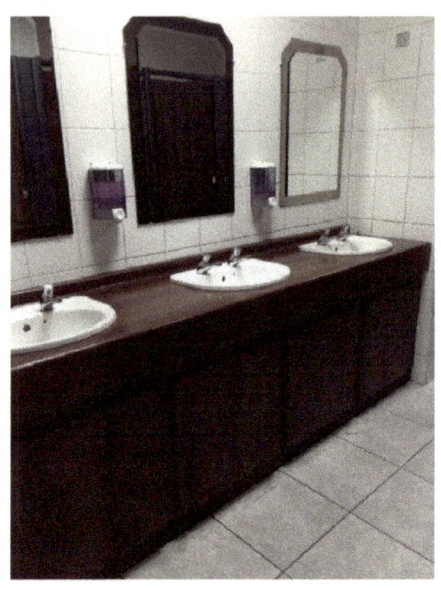

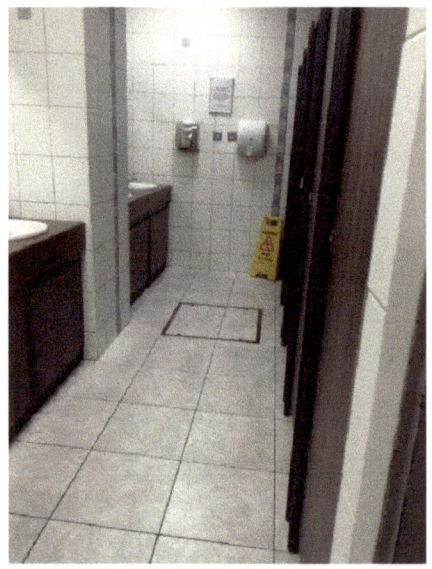

Establishments have certainly gotten creative in the way they inform patrons which bathroom is for which gender.

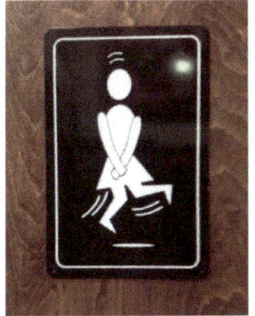 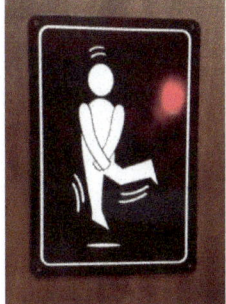 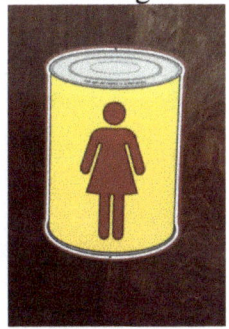

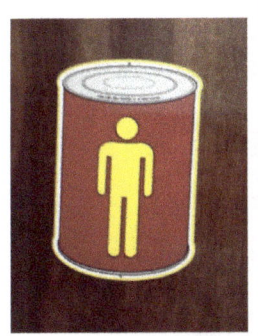 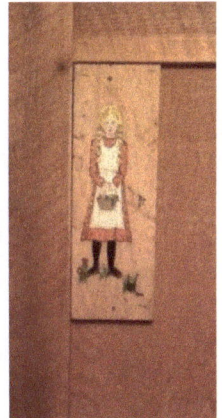 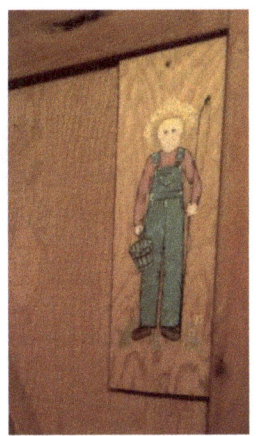

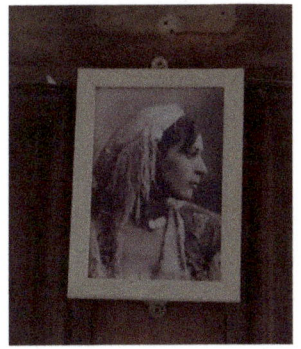 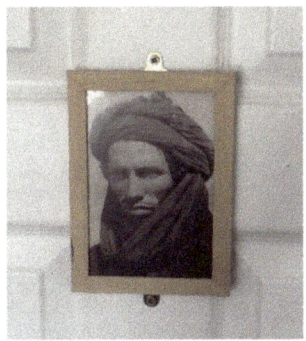

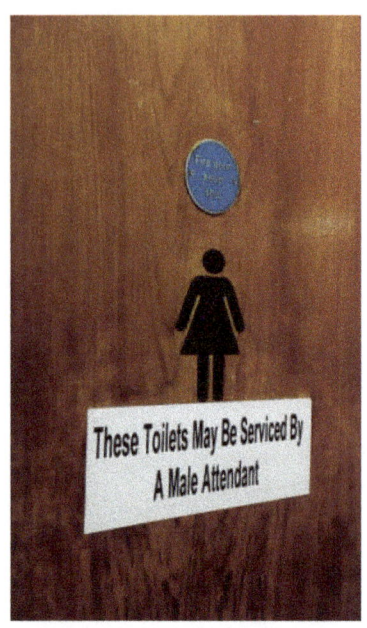

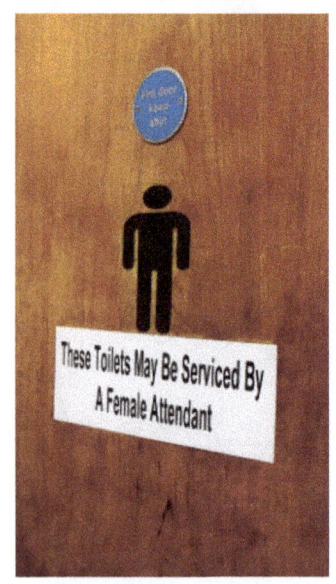

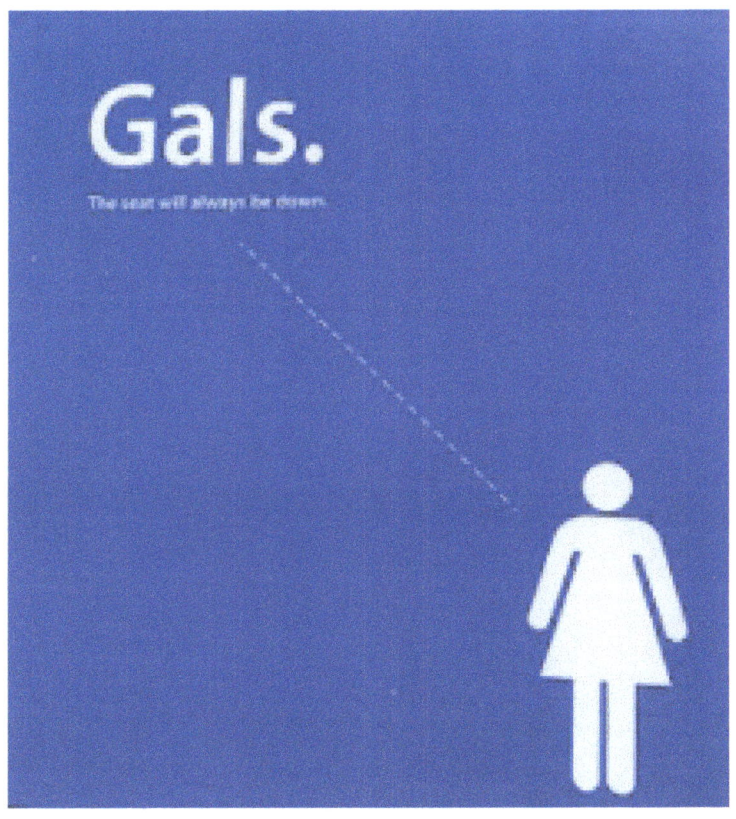

In case you can't read the text below "gals," it reads, "The seat will always be down."

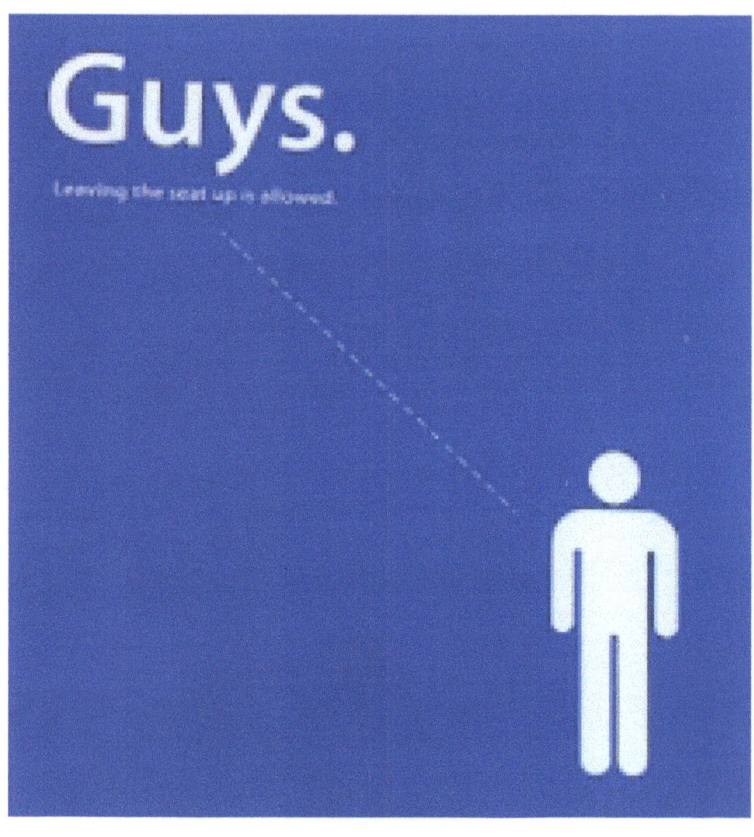

In case you can't read the text below "guys," it reads,
"Leaving the seat up is allowed."

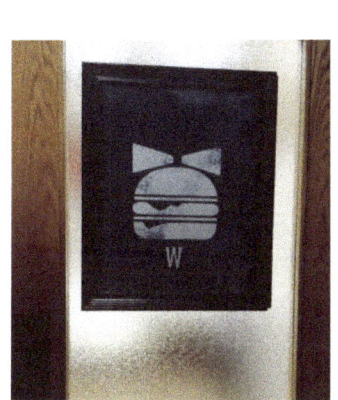

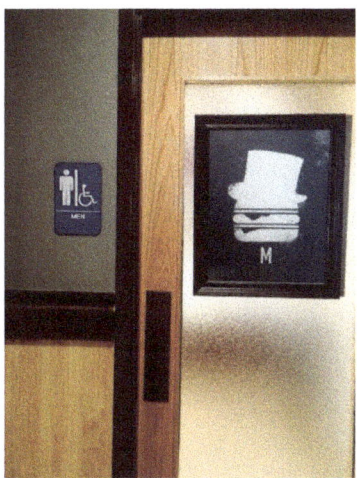

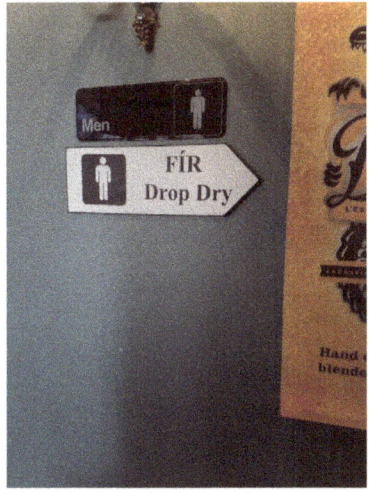

* * *

In case you missed the voluntary collection box on the desk, just outside the toilet entrance, where a parishioner is almost always seated, here's a reminder.

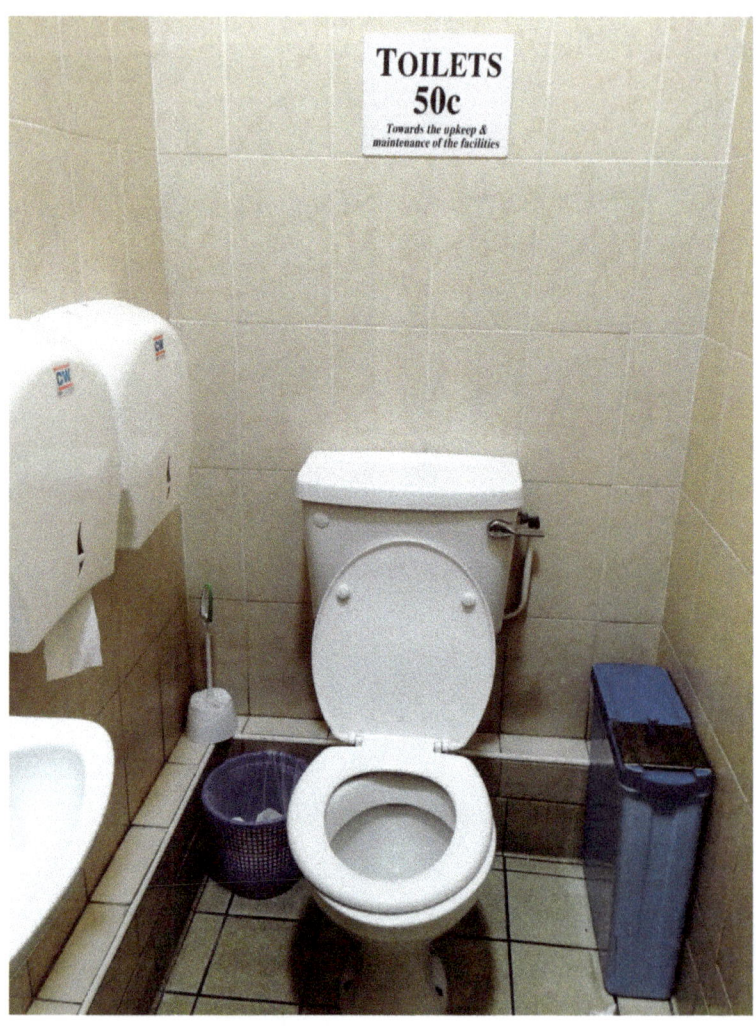

I was always so grateful for this halfway stopping point to empty my bladder between town and my B&B while studying in Ireland that I usually dropped in more than a 50 cent coin.

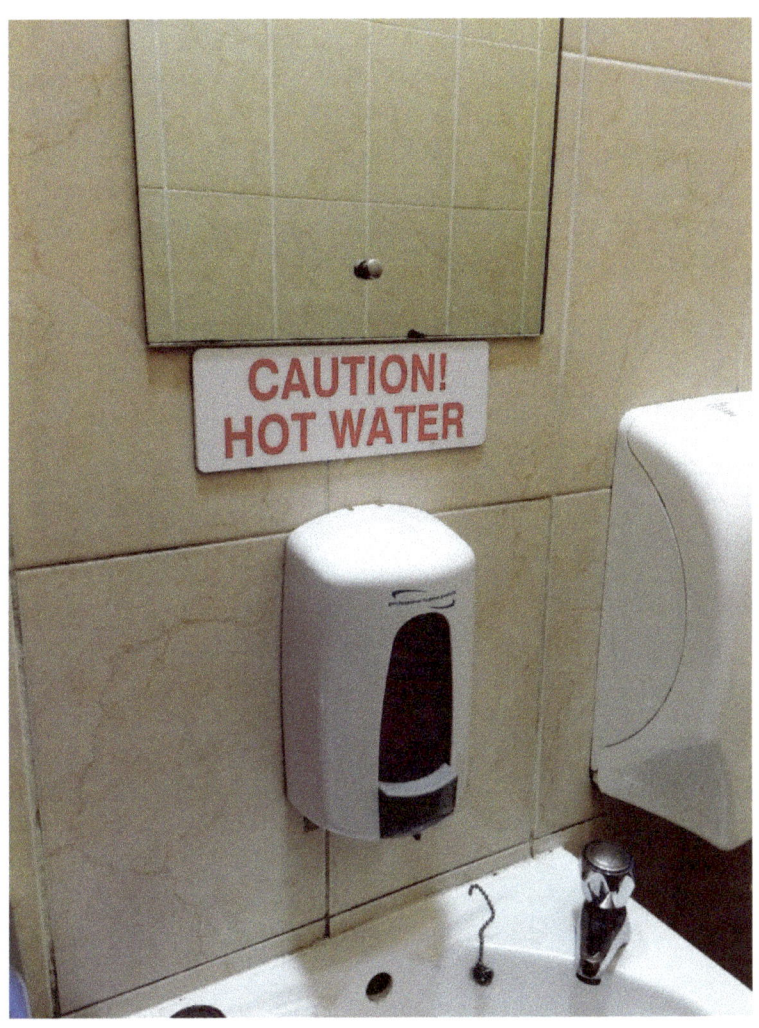

No mistake there about the water temperature.

When I was at Galway's St. Nicholas' church (famed for being the last place Christopher Columbus received mass before setting off for the new world), attending a wonderful concert of traditional Irish music and dance, I felt the urge to empty my bladder at intermission. This was the only available toilet on the property. And it looked private... enough...

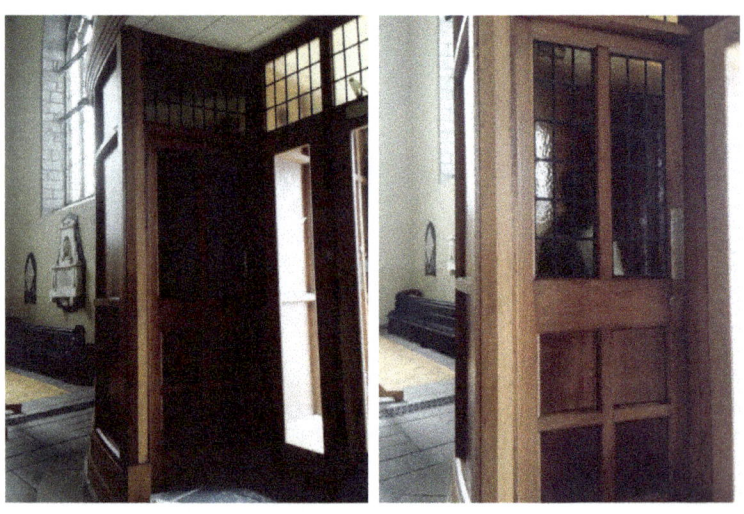

...until the lights were turned on. That's my son behind the glass. Spooky how much you can see, and how far one has to go inside the toilet to not be seen.

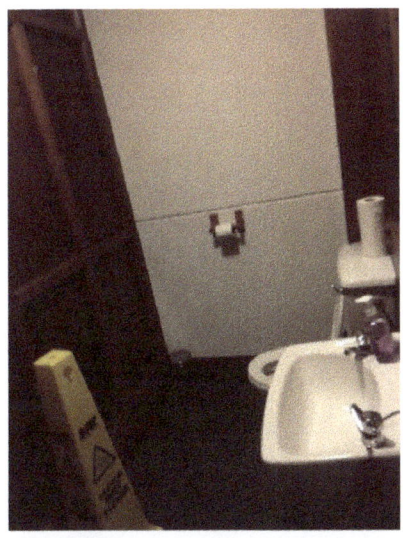

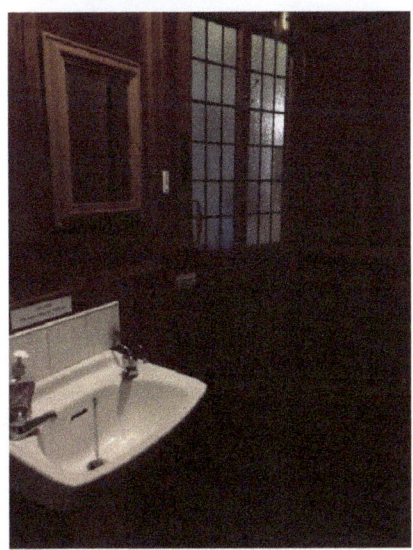

I'm surprised no one noticed me taking pictures. Now, I know people in church want to know your business, but isn't this a bit much!?

One of the things I loved best about toilets in Ireland was the feminine product disposal system they have. Ladies, you know what it's like, to have to take care of such an inconvenient thing and to be in a public stall where other females weren't as tidy at disposal as you are. It can be quite sickening to deal with these receptacles we find in our stalls more often than not. But look at what they use! It's less like a disgusting chore, more of a pleasant deposit, like at a bank drop off window. You don't have to touch it, just use your foot!

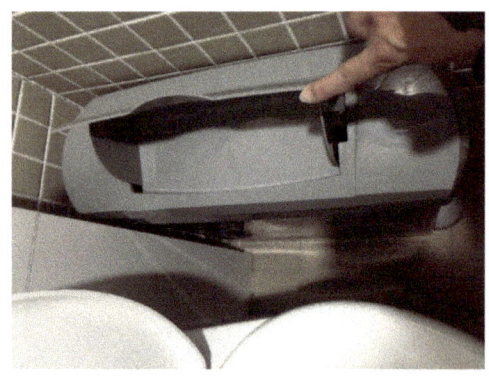

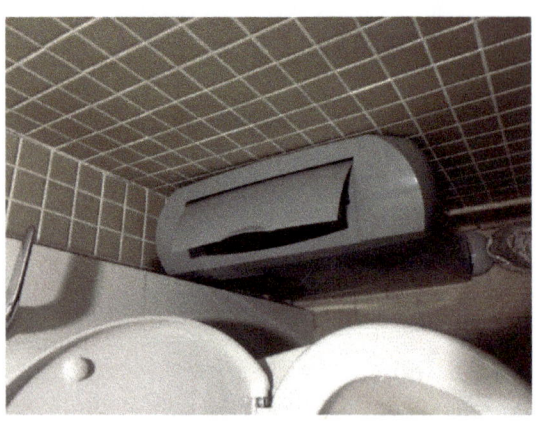

And while I have your attention, ladies, what about the age-old problem of what to do with our purses. I have come across some interesting storage solutions in my travels.

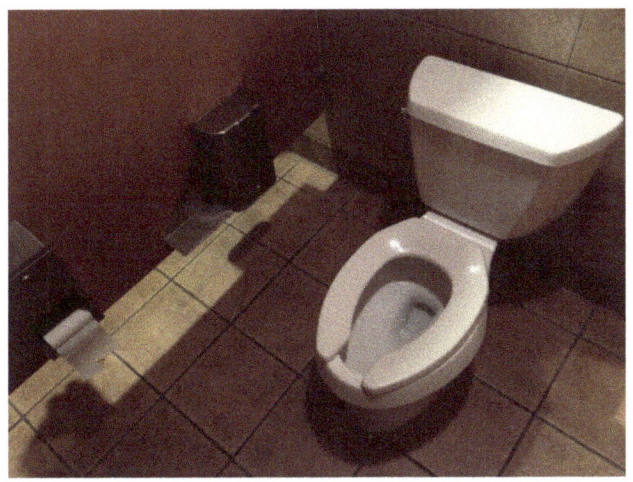

Here is a shelf attached to the afore-mentioned hygiene receptacle that's not so hygienic. Multiples…

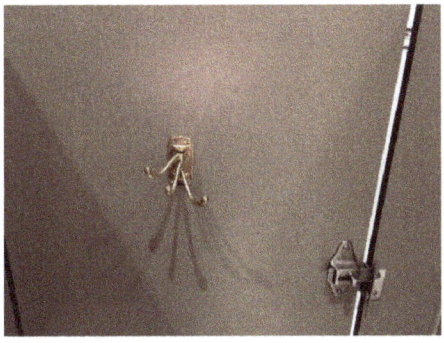

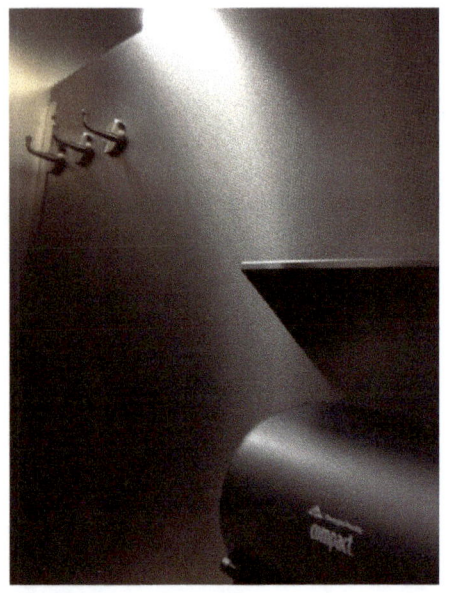

and if the hooks aren't enough, there's a shelf too.

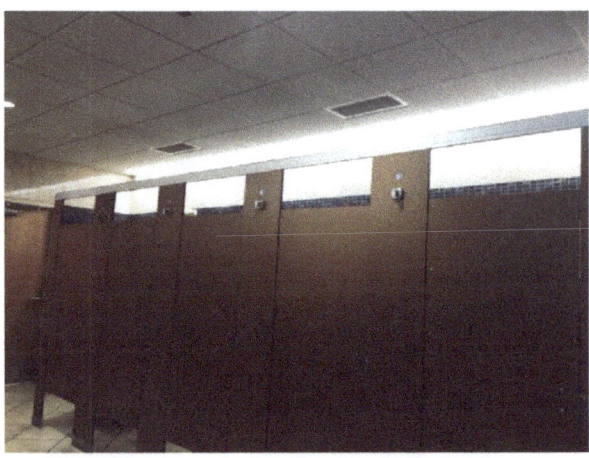

Granted, this was at an airport, but still I'm not surprised at all that this bathroom was a full house and not one lady followed these directions.

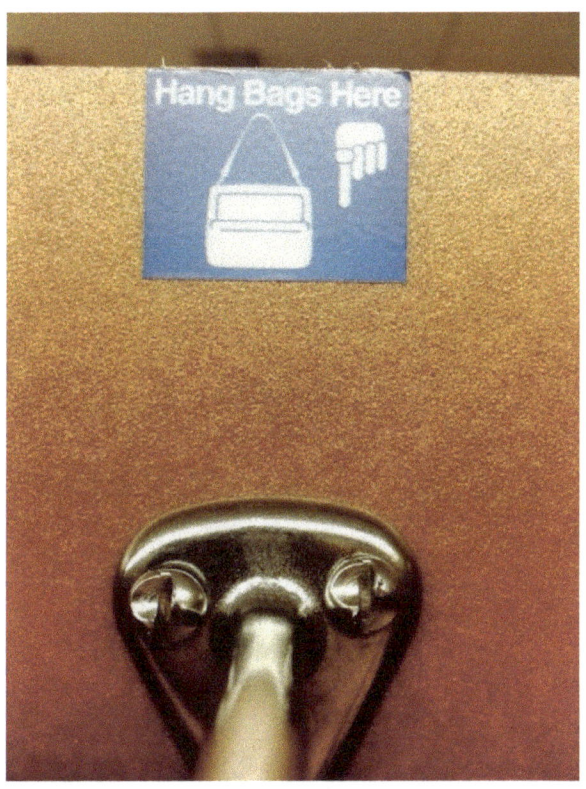

Here we go, better placement of the purse,
where you need it to be when on the throne.

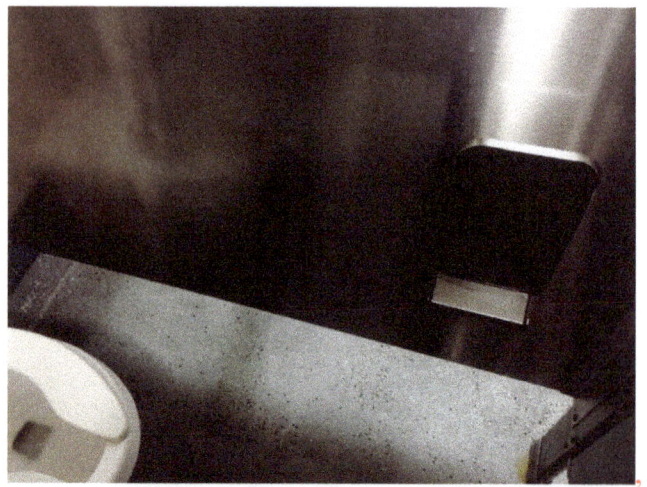

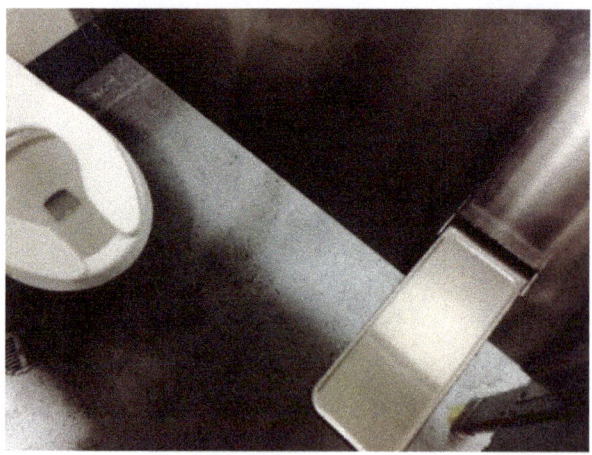

In Ireland they are getting the idea, that a lady
needs her purse close at hand always.

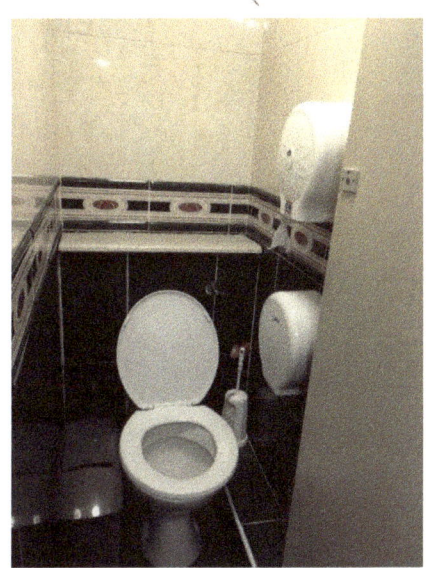

And not to be outdone, even a posh restaurant cares about its lady patrons' needs.

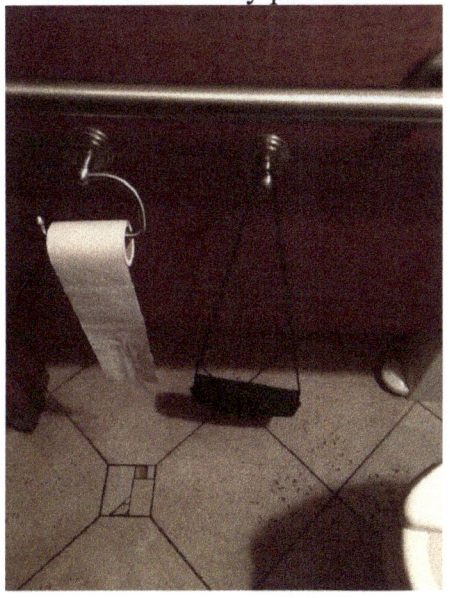

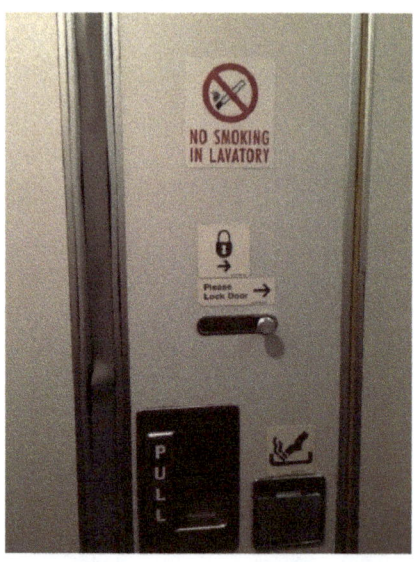

No smoking allowed? So, why is there an ashtray??

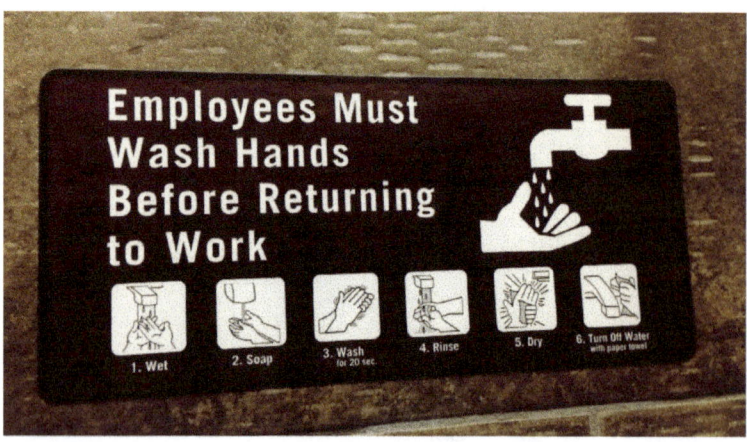

This establishment wanted to make sure their employees not only knew to wash their hands, but specifically how to as well.

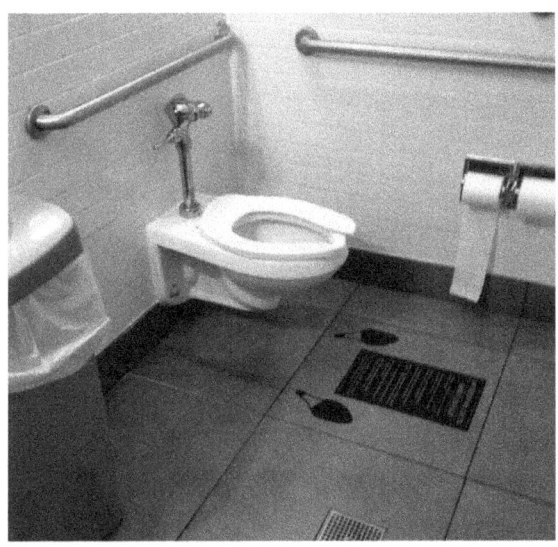

This fast food restaurant likes to be very entertaining, even in their patrons' solitary moments. Whimsically placed, but informative, says this former science teacher.

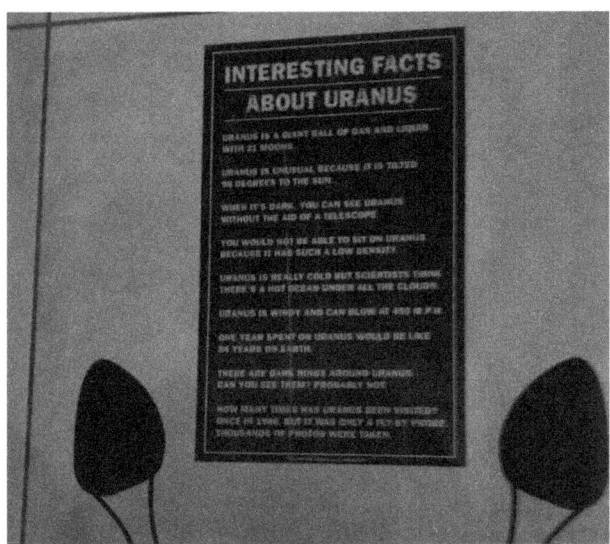

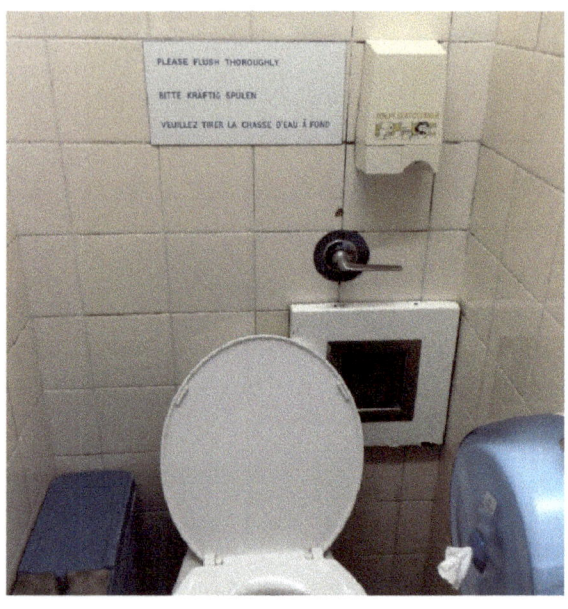

As if you didn't get enough toilet cleaning at home, here, do it while you're on vacation in a foreign country.

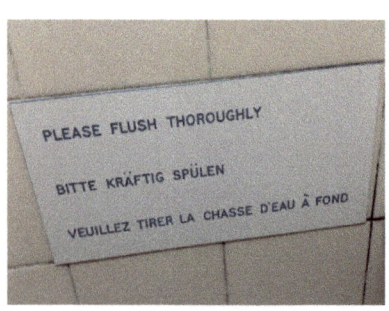

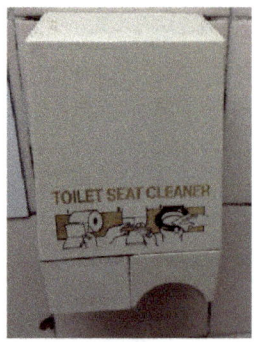

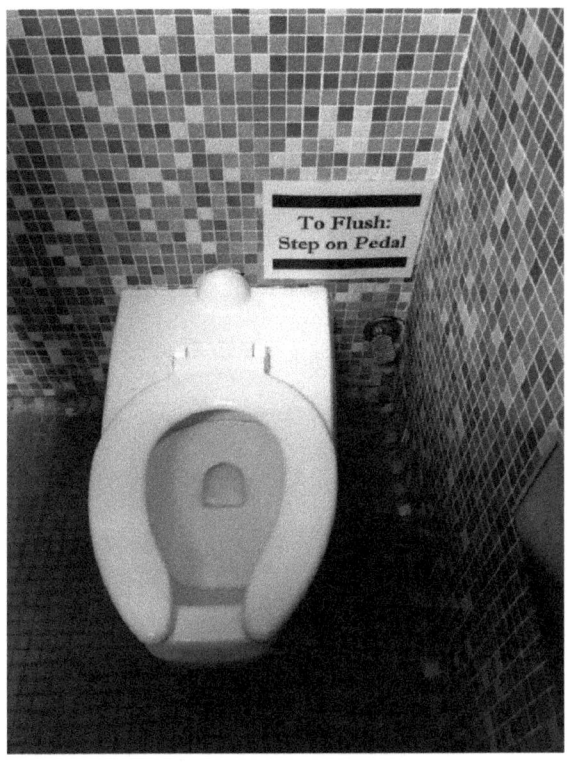

To Flush:
Step on Pedal

I wouldn't have known otherwise. I might still be standing there trying to find the flusher.

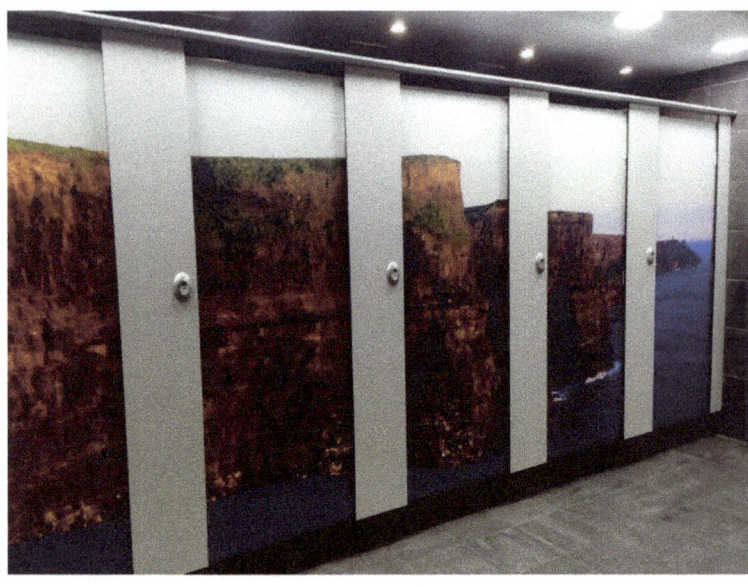

Just so you don't forget where you are when you pop to the loo. Or was this mural done so you could still see the view while waiting in line and you didn't miss your tour bus back?

The tour bus company said there was a toilet on the bus. Let's play "Where's the Loo?"

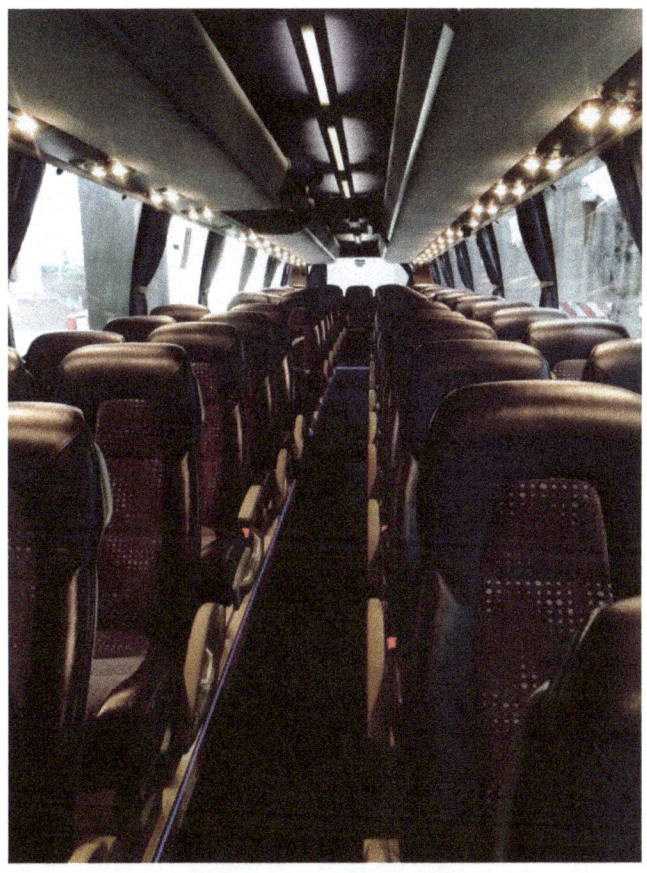

"In the middle," the bus driver directed. So I made my way toward the back, dubious I'd see the facility I so desperately needed.

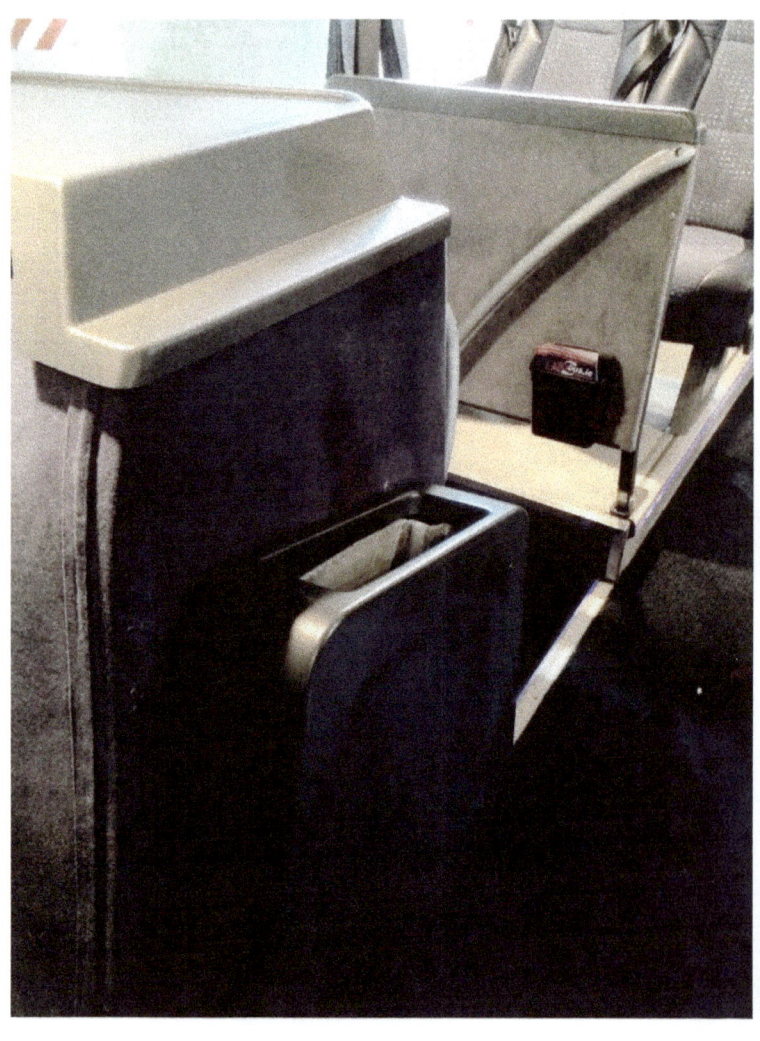

Sure enough.

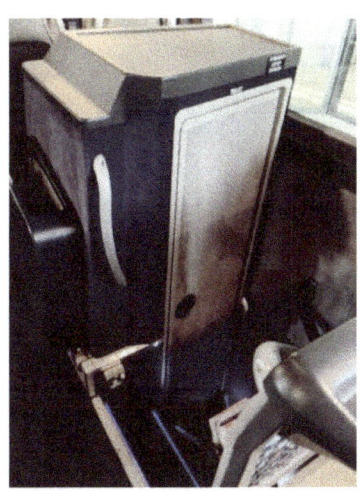

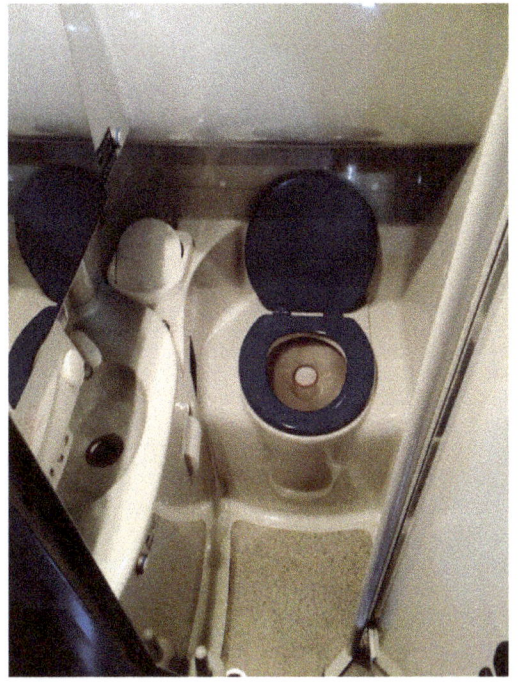

After all the other passengers had disembarked, I told the bus driver that I was writing a book…a book about toilets…and wondered if he minded me staying onboard a few moments longer to get some pictures of the loo. I'm so glad he was thrilled with the idea of his bus toilet being featured in this book.

* * *

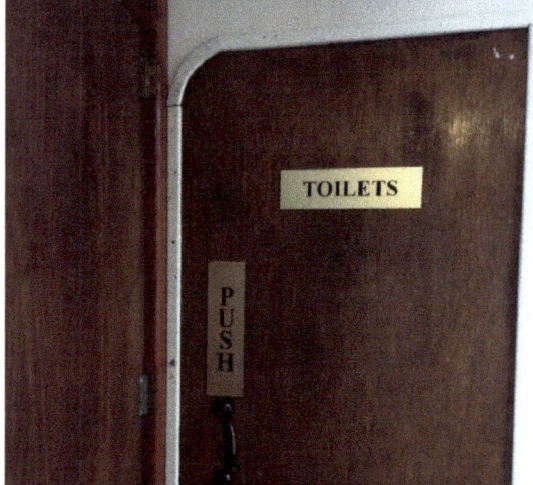

What's the fist thing you want to find before the boat departs the dock? The toilet. But, the sign lied, there was only one seat. And why is the lock on the outside of the door?

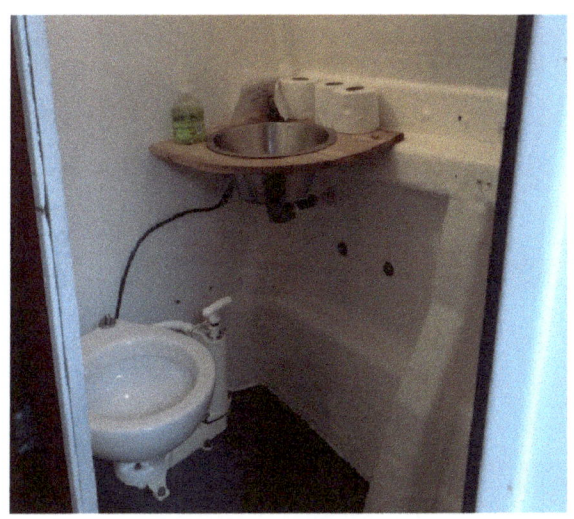

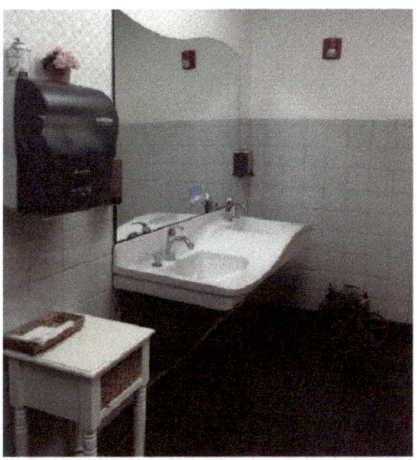

I'm getting seasick just from looking
at the wave of this sink.

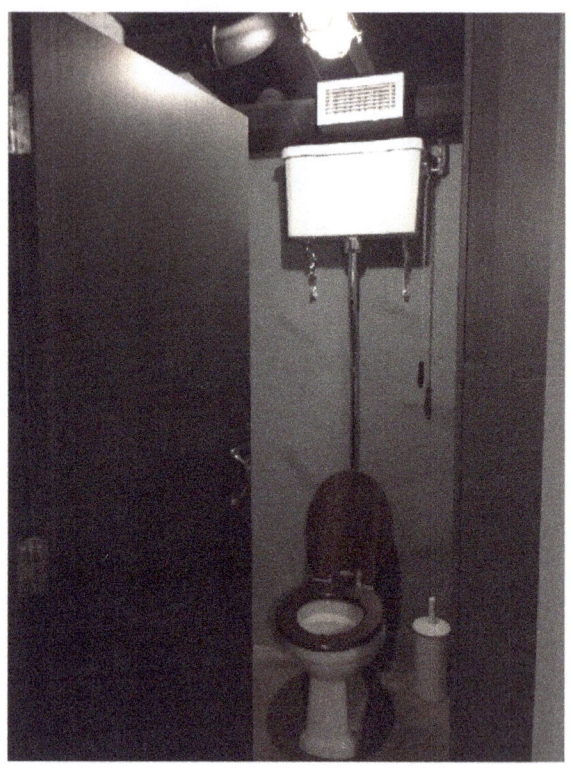

I didn't know they actually made this style anymore. And yes, it did flush as the old ones did a century or so ago.

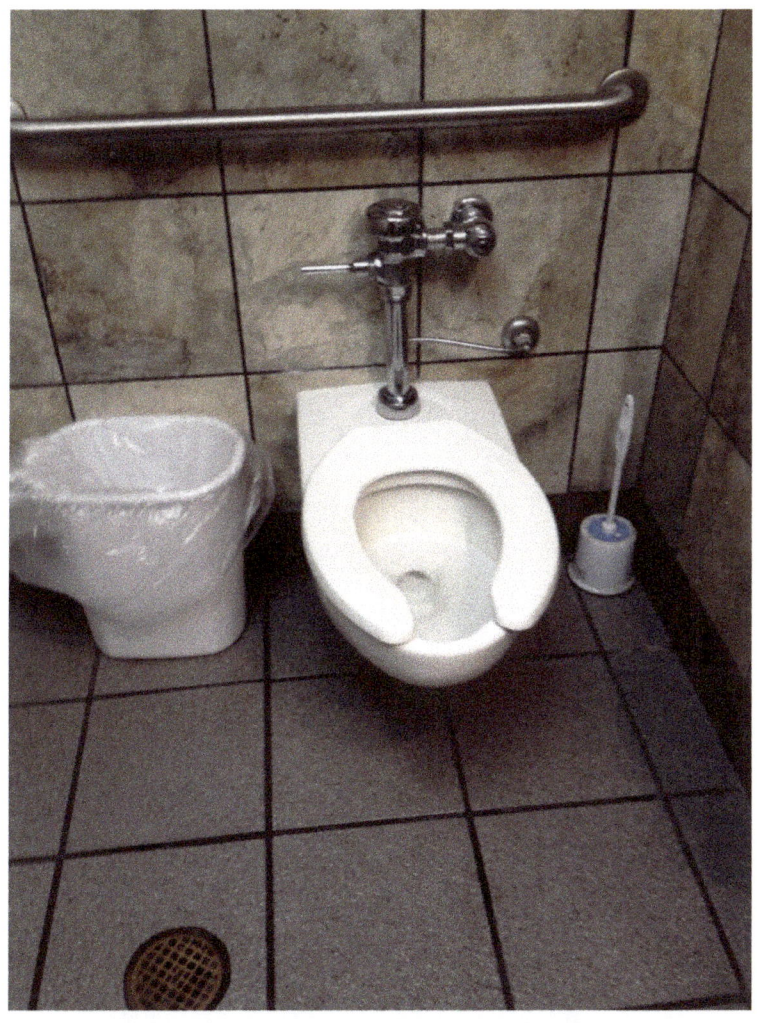

I'm vertically challenged, but this seat was set too low for even me!

The strangest thing I think I have ever seen
has been a sideways toilet stall.

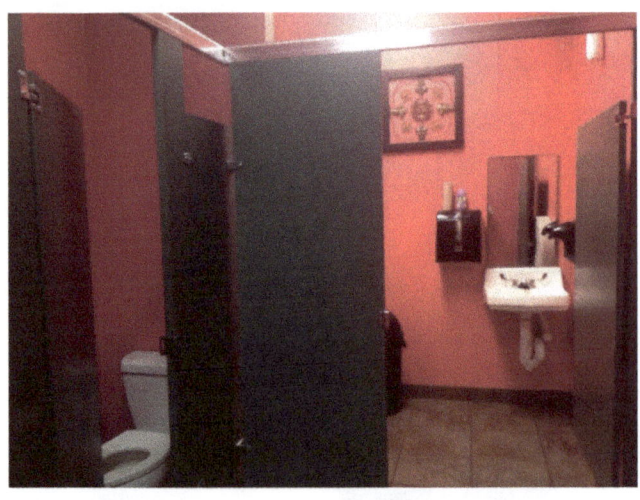

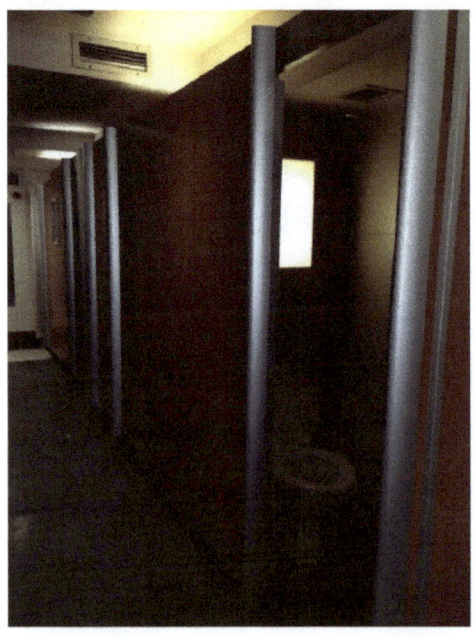

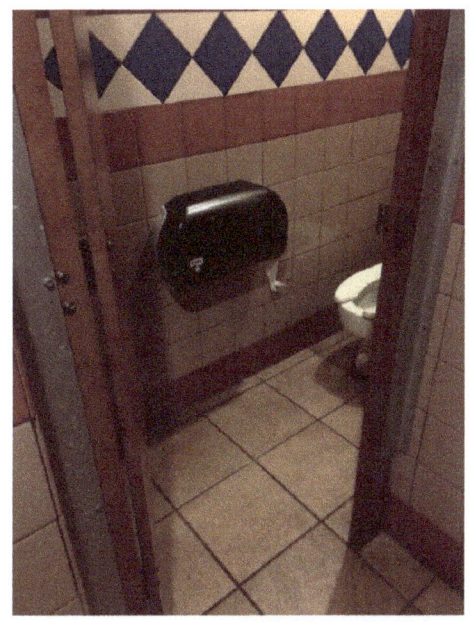

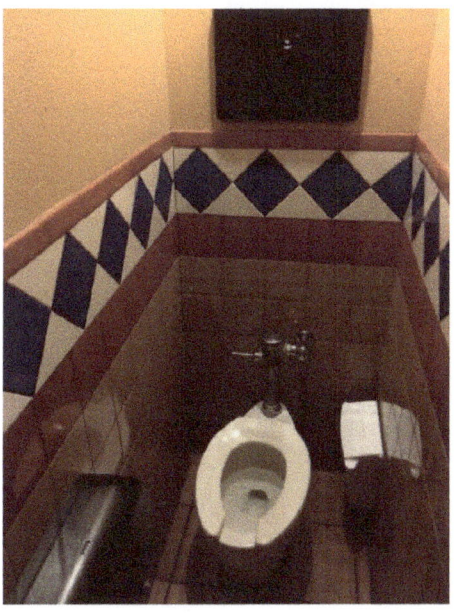

But one must be very careful when deciding how to face the opposing toilets in adjoining stalls. Our friends in Ireland take toilet privacy very seriously and build their stall walls very solid and almost always from ceiling to floor.

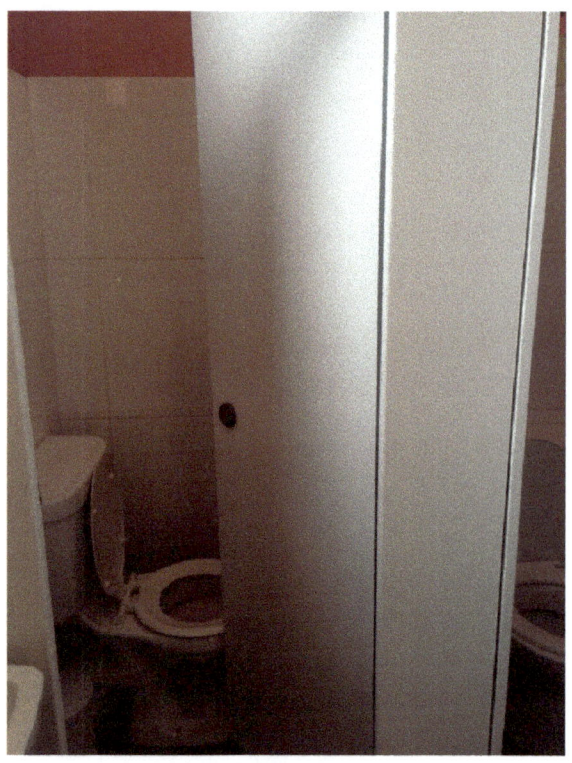

However, here in America, where the stall walls are not so well constructed, it's not the best idea to have the sideways toilet facing the toilet it is perpendicular to.

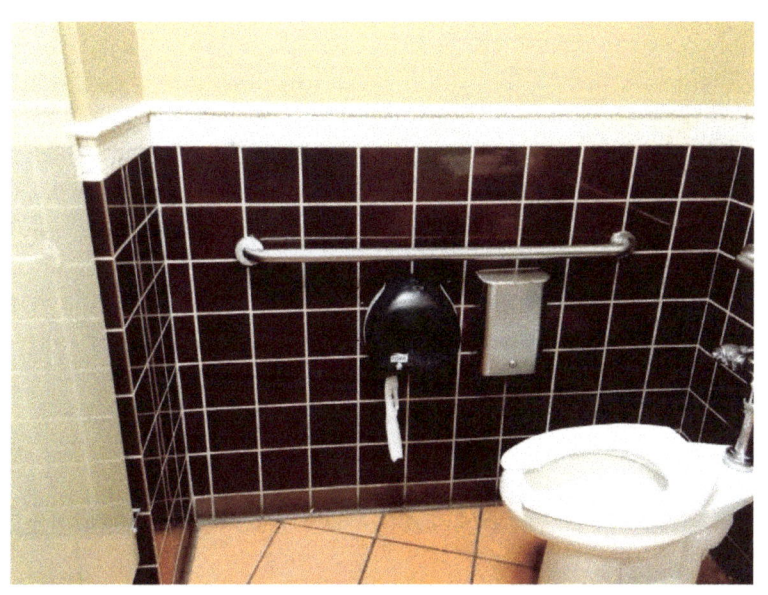

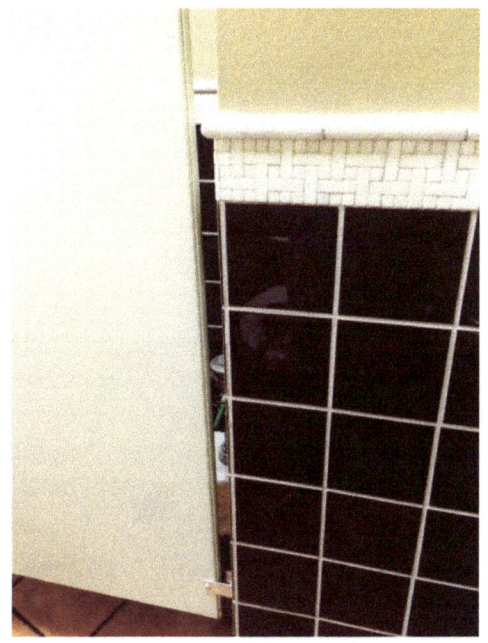

I was out to lunch with a group of coworkers when I heard nature calling me. I went into the sideways toilet (p. 103) not thinking anything of it, but having sat down to do my business I then looked up, as you do, and through the sizable gap, I saw the back side of one of those ladies was sharing a meal with! I had to wait a long time to be able to snap the picture. I hope she didn't look through any of the other gaps around the stall and see me dallying in there with my camera poised.

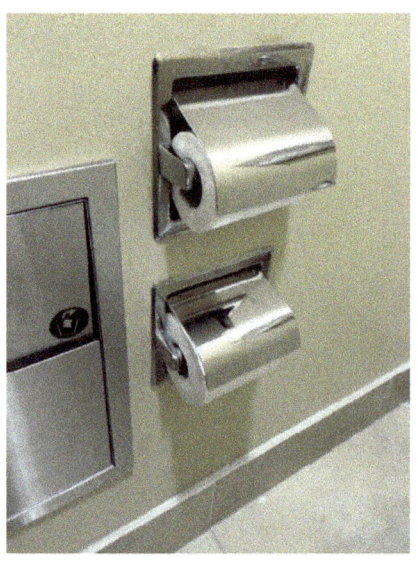

In Japan, it was common, at least in household bathrooms, to see a toilet paper roll holder with a metal flap over top. I think it has something to do with managing the amount of toilet paper used at each sitting. Maybe the harder you tug at the roll the fewer sheets you will take, perhaps? But, I had not ever seen this style in America before I visited this church toilet.

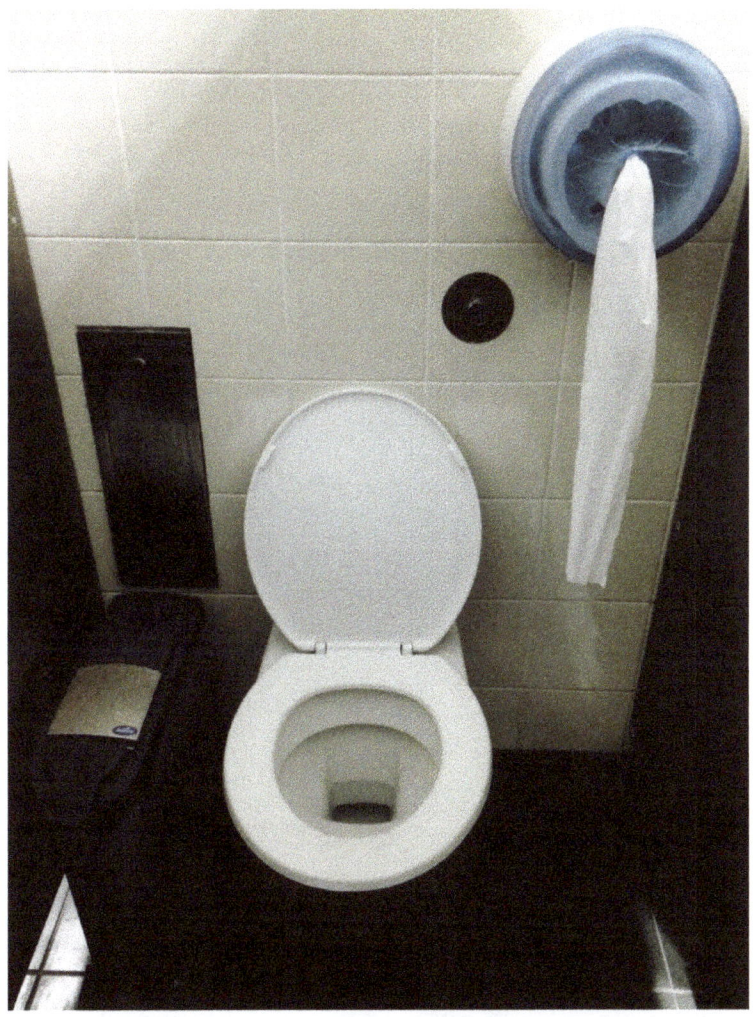

You have to admit, this style of dispensing toilet paper is ingenious. The roll unravels from the inside out. What isn't so brilliant though, if you want to keep your shoulder in its socket, is the placement of this dispenser.

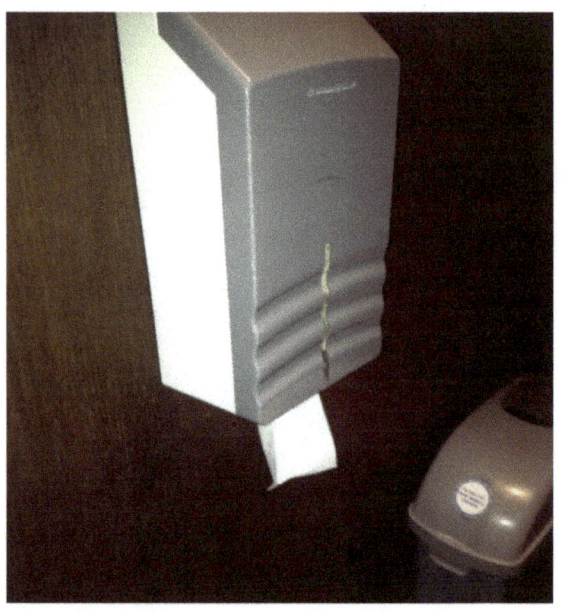

It was more like a paper towel dispenser than toilet tissue, and yes, it yielded exactly one sheet each time you tugged.

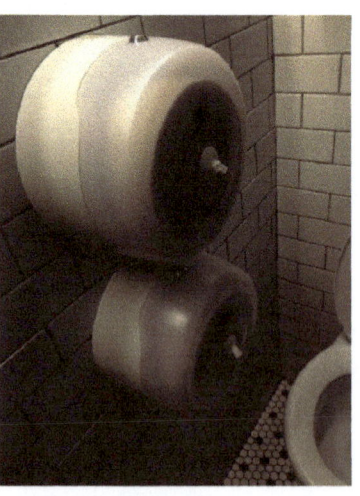

I think I will sit back on this one and just let you have fun coming up with your own commentary. You could try turning the book to one side to get started. You're welcome.

And for my publisher...

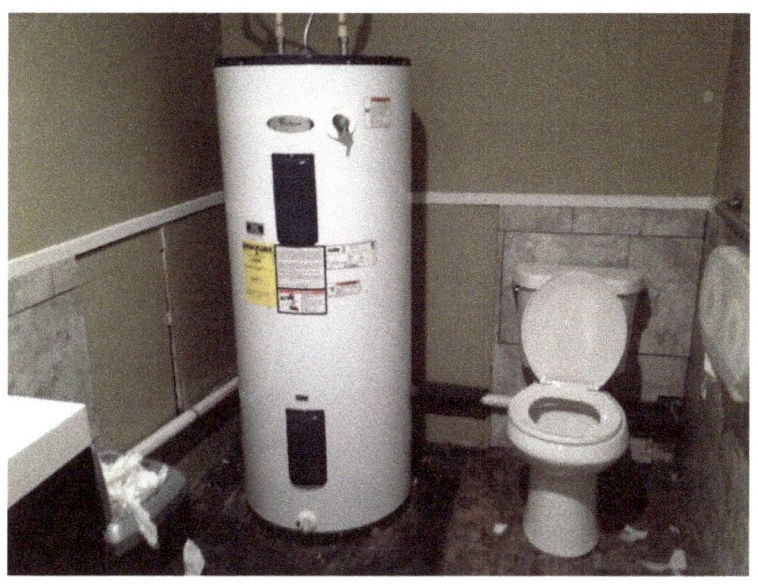

a messy toilet that I actually used and didn't run from
screaming.

ACKNOWLEDGMENTS

The author would like to acknowledge the following
people for their various contributions to this book: Pam,
Sandra, Debi, Sean, Ron, Carl, and Peter.

www.ingramcontent.com/pod-product-compliance
Lightning Source LLC
Chambersburg PA
CBHW040952170526
45159CB00013B/3110